I0083450

MEL C. MULLEN

YOU CHOOSE

12 DECISIONS TO SHAPE YOUR LIFE

MCHJ VENTURES INC.

You Choose: 12 Decisions to Shape Your Life
© 2026 by Mel Mullen

Published by MCHJ Ventures Inc.

ISBN 978-1-963127-48-5
Ebook 978-1-963127-49-2

Cover design by Pablo Becker-Lozano

Scripture copyrights:
NLT: New Living Translation. Copyright © 1996, 2004, 2007 by Tyndale House Foundation. Used by permission of Tyndale House Publishers, Inc., Carol Stream, Illinois 60188. All rights reserved.
ESV: English Standard Version®. Copyright © 2001 by Crossway, a publishing ministry of Good News Publishers. All rights reserved.
NCV: New Century Version®. Copyright © 2005 by Thomas Nelson. Used by permission. All rights reserved.
NIV: New International Version®. Copyright © 1973, 1978, 1984, 2011 by Biblica, Inc. Used by permission of Zondervan. All rights reserved.
NKJV: New King James Version®. Copyright © 1982 by Thomas Nelson, Inc. Used by permission. All rights reserved.
KJV: King James Version. Public domain.
TPT: The Passion Translation®. Copyright © 2017, 2018, 2020 by Passion & Fire Ministries, Inc. Used by permission. All rights reserved.
MSG: The Message. Copyright © 1993–2002 by Eugene H. Peterson. Used by permission of NavPress Publishing Group, a division of The Navigators. All rights reserved.
AMP: Amplified® Bible. Copyright © 2015 by The Lockman Foundation. Used by permission. All rights reserved.
NASB: New American Standard Bible®. Copyright © 1960, 1971, 1977, 1995, 2020 by The Lockman Foundation. All rights reserved.

Worldwide rights reserved. No part of this publication may be reproduced, stored in a retrieval system, or transmitted, in any form or by any means, without written consent from the publisher. The views and opinions expressed herein are solely those of the author and not necessarily those of the publishers.

Printed in Canada

PRAISE FOR *YOU CHOOSE*

My dad, Mel Mullen, founder of Home Church, has always carried a strong desire to empower young leaders and see them succeed. Making the right choices was a common theme in how my father and mother raised me and how they built our church. Life was always about developing a Christ-like character as we chose to live Christ's way. *You Choose* is a book that empowers young people to walk the walk and live in God's way, according to His Word. It will help any person navigate life's decisions with clarity and conviction. Making the right decisions will not only help you succeed but also give you the tools you need to avoid life's dangerous pitfalls. This book is a must-read for young people, as well as for anyone who desires to follow God's call on their life.

— Jachin Mullen, Lead Pastor of Home Church, Red Deer AB

"You Choose is more than a book, it's a biblical roadmap for life in a world that has become increasingly difficult to navigate. I have witnessed that Mel carries the heart of a pastor and the wisdom of a father, and both shine through in this powerful book. Just as Christ chose twelve disciples, this book gives you twelve choices that will define the outcome of your days on earth and echo into eternity. Each chapter blends biblical truth, personal story, and practical reflection in a way that speaks directly to this rising generation. A must-read!"

— Ryan McVety, Lead Pastor at The River Worship

To my grandchildren:

Jade and Kaleb Furst
Davin Carritt
Levi Justice Mullen
Ava Grace Mullen
Jude Jachin Mullen
Matthew Jackson Mullen

...and the generations of family yet to come.

CONTENTS

FOREWORD

by Pastor Manny Arango

Every generation eventually discovers that a meaningful life is never accidental. Scripture reveals that whenever God speaks, order emerges from chaos, and whenever His voice is ignored, chaos returns. The opening lines of Genesis present this with remarkable clarity. The world begins in a state of tohu va vohu, a Hebrew phrase that conveys confusion and disarray. The Spirit hovers over the deep and the voice of God establishes boundaries, distinctions, and rhythms. Scholars note that this narrative is not primarily an explanation of material origins. It is a portrait of how divine wisdom transforms disorder into x.

This movement from chaos to order is not confined to the creation story. It becomes a recurring pattern throughout the Bible. Chaos appears. Waters rise. The Spirit moves. God speaks. Order is restored. Then comes a test. Humanity either partners with God in sustaining order or drifts back toward chaos. The cycle repeats through Noah, the exodus, the wilderness, the promised land, and finally in the life of Jesus. When Jesus endures the wilderness test, He breaks the cycle and makes it possible for humanity to walk in the order and peace that God intended from the beginning.

I raise this pattern because the next generation faces a cultural landscape where chaos often feels normal. Many young people are encouraged to live reactively rather than intentionally. Yet Scripture consistently teaches that disorder gains ground wherever intentional choices are neglected. Chaos does not need to be invited. It only needs to be unchallenged.

This is what makes Mel Mullen's You Choose so timely and important. It calls young leaders to recognize that every decision carries spiritual weight. The book does not offer sentimental advice. It offers a biblical framework for understanding how choices shape character, direction, and destiny. Its blend of story, Scripture, testimony, and reflection creates space for readers to consider the internal order of their lives with honesty and depth.

In Crushing Chaos I wrote that God created a good world, not a flawless one. He tamed enough chaos to make life possible, and He entrusted humanity with the responsibility to cultivate the rest. The same principle guides the life of every believer. God provides His Spirit and His Word, yet He leaves room for our agency. Intentionality becomes a form of worship. Choosing well is how we participate in God's ongoing work of ordering creation.

My hope is that as you engage these chapters you begin to see your decisions as sacred acts. You are shaping the atmosphere of your inner world. You are either aligning your life with the structure God designed or allowing chaos to be reintroduced through inattention or compromise.

May the Holy Spirit grant you clarity as you read. May your choices reflect the wisdom of God. And may the order He cultivates within you become a testimony of His peace in a chaotic age.

Choose well.

—Pastor Manny Arango

INTRODUCTION
THE POWER OF CHOICE

"Now choose life, so that you and your children may live."
Deuteronomy 30:19 (NIV)

If I could sit across from every teenager and young adult, I would talk with you about the years between 16 and 24. These years carry a weight you may not fully see yet. This season is a foundation for the rest of your life. The decisions you make now about faith, friendships, habits, identity, purity, and purpose will change everything.

Every young person reaches a crossroads where intention is no longer enough. At some point, you must move your life from good intentions to bold decisions—choices that shape your future, set the direction of your calling, and determine who you become.

Sadly, many young people drift through these years without direction, wasting opportunities and setting their lives on paths that lead to regret. But it doesn't have to be that way. God has given you the power of choice.

You Choose is written for you, and also for every parent, mentor, and grandparent who longs to see the next generation rise strong. Each chapter includes a story from my own journey, timeless biblical principles, scriptures about the topic, a testimony from a young leader who is living out these truths today, and questions designed to help you reflect deeply and honestly.

This book isn't just information—it's an invitation. It's a conversation we will walk through together as you learn how to make the kind of choices that build a great life. So let's explore these questions one by one.

1. **God's Perfect Will**: Why is God's plan the best plan for your life?

2. **Identity**: Why did God form you, call you, and give you purpose?

3. **Obedience**: Why should you obey God and trust what He says?

4. **Friends**: How do the friends you choose today shape your tomorrow?

5. **Purity**: Why does moral purity protect your heart and future?

6. **Truth**: How can you choose truth when deception is all around you?

7. **More Than Enough**: Why live in lack when God designed you for abundance and a prosperous life?

8. **Disciplines**: How can you bring discipline and order into your daily habits?

9. **Confidence**: Why let insecurity rule you when God calls you to live with confidence?

10. **Enjoy Life**: Why live empty when God invites you to enjoy life fully and joyfully?

11. Be a Leader: Why did God create you to lead and influence others?

12. Win and Never Quit: How can you become a winner in life?

These are the choices that build a life worth living. These are the decisions that shape your destiny. And these are the truths I pray you'll carry with you for the rest of your journey.

—Mel C. Mullen

CHOICE 1
GOD'S WILL

Life is not perfect, but God has a perfect plan for your life.

MY STORY

When I was seventeen years old, I was a very sincere follower of Jesus. I believed God had a plan for my life. My favourite passage of scripture was Romans 12:2. "Don't copy the behaviour and customs of this world, but let God transform you into a new person by changing the way you think. Then you will learn to know God's will for you, which is good and pleasing and perfect" (NLT).

I had just graduated from grade 12, and I urgently needed to decide about my future. Would I go to a trade school? University? Do something entirely different? I prayed and asked the Lord to show me His plan for my life.

A good friend suggested I write a list of all my potential career paths and put stars beside the options that most interested me. Five stars meant that I really wanted that possibility, while one star meant it was a less desirable option for the future.

I created a list—a very long one, I remember—and put stars next to each option, according to how I felt about each one. The list included things like doctor, lawyer, teacher, mechanic, accountant, manager of a company, and more.

Then, I decided to take that long list to summer camp and ask God to give me direction for my life. I believed He would tell me which of these options was His perfect will for me.

At the conclusion of one of the camp services, I boldly walked forward, laid the paper on a wooden altar, knelt, and prayed: "Lord, what is your will for my life?"

I was expecting God to direct me to one of the choices on the paper, but suddenly I heard an inner voice speaking to me.

"Son," said the voice, "I have a work for you to do."

Right then, I knew God had spoken to me. It was crystal clear, like when the finger of God wrote words on the stone tablets that became the Ten Commandments.

This pivotal moment of my life immediately began to shape my future. I knew immediately what I had to do: enrol in the Full Gospel Bible Institute in Eston, Saskatchewan and pursue God's call on my life.

So I stood up, walked confidently out of the meeting, found my mother, and announced, "I'm going to enrol in the Bible college. I believe I am called to be a minister."

With those eight words from the Lord—*I have a work for you to do*—I knew that God would guide me into my life purpose and lead me into a wonderful future. God had a perfect plan for my life and I could set my future according to His will.

WHAT DO YOU THINK GOD'S PLAN IS FOR YOUR LIFE?

I can't answer that question for you, but I can promise you this: God's plan is good and perfect. Too often, the vision many of us are given for our lives is too small, too negative, and too mediocre.

A while back, I introduced my grandson to the owner of a prominent business in Red Deer and said, "I am so proud of Levi. He is making right choices in his life that will lead him to a great, successful future."

The manager replied, "Levi, I have some good advice for you. Just buy yourself some time. You are young. Just don't do drugs, don't get drunk, don't get some girl pregnant, and don't go to jail, and everything will be alright for you."

As we left the business, I thought, *Isn't there more to life than just "Don't do stupid things"? Isn't it made up of making wise choices that determine the future?*

Instead of settling for a life that is just about not doing dumb things, let's go to the Word of God and see what He says.

> "For I know the plans and thoughts that I have for you," says the Lord, "plans for peace and well-being and not for disaster, to give you a future and a hope" (Jeremiah 29:11–13 AMP).

This verse is even more powerful when you understand the context in which it was written. Young people of the day were torn from their families, kidnapped, and taken to the foreign city of Babylon, where they became refugees in the Babylonian re-training programme. Everything they knew was gone and their circumstances looked hopeless—but God had a plan for every one of them.

These youth became our Biblical heroes, Daniel, Esther, Shadrach, Meshach, Abednego, Ezra, Nehemiah, and Zerubbabel.

- Daniel ended up advising kings.
- Esther became queen of Persia and saved her entire nation.
- Shadrach, Meshach, and Abednego walked through fire, survived the blazing furnace, and showed us what uncompromised faith looks like.
- Ezra and Zerubbabel returned to rebuild the temple of God.
- Nehemiah returned to rebuild the walls of Jerusalem.

Each of them had a unique calling, and they walked right into it—not by accident, but by God's design.

The scripture I quoted above was a prophecy given seventy years before these young people were torn away from their families, friends, and country, and carried away captive. Through the prophetic words spoken by Jeremiah the prophet, God gave them a promise that His people would return to their homeland. God knew their future was greater than the dilemma or the circumstances they would face in the land of their captivity.

God has a great plan for your future too! Here are some questions for you to consider.

1. **Will I base my life on choices I make for myself, or will I allow God to direct my future?**

People often set the course of their life and then ask God to bless their plans, but that's backwards. We should start with God's will and blessing, then set our lives based on that.

Jesus is the perfect example of this. He lived according to a prophetic scripture written about Him: "I take joy in doing your will, my God, for your instructions are written on my heart" (Psalm 40:8 NLT).

Jesus Himself, when He was talking about God's plan for Him: "Yet not as I will, but as you will" (Matthew 26:39 NIV).

2. **When did God set a plan for my future?**

According to the book of Jeremiah, God chose you before the foundation of the world. That's when He mapped out your future ahead of you.

"Before I made you in your mother's womb, I chose you. Before you were born, I set you apart for a special work. I appointed you as a prophet to the nations" (Jeremiah 1:5 NCV).

Can you believe that? Before the foundation of the world, before God formed the first person from the dust of the ground and breathed into him the breath of life, He mapped out a plan for your life. He knew when you would be born, where you would live, and what decisions you would make.

3.   What if I have already made too many choices that have taken me in the wrong direction?

The good news is that God is a God of grace. He knew the mistakes you would make, and He has a plan to get you back into His perfect will for your future.

4.   How can I know that I am in God's perfect will for my life?

Just as you can know that you are saved, you can have the confidence that you are walking in the perfect will of God for your life.

You might ask, "But what if I make a mistake?"

Remember Peter walking on water? He had to get out of the boat first. Was he scared? Of course. Did he have all the answers? Not at all. But he knew Jesus' voice, and that was enough. And by the way—he did sink, but Jesus didn't let him drown. His grace was enough for Peter's weakness, and it will be enough for you.

The Bible is clear: you are not an accident or a victim of random circumstances. You have to believe that! From before your first breath, God had a future in mind for you. He built your personality, gave you talents, and allowed you to experience certain things. Nothing about you is an accident, and nothing you have gone through up until now is a waste.

Maybe you're feeling anxious about your future right now. Maybe you feel like you're lost in the fog, stumbling from one thing to the next, with no definitive direction.

Or maybe you're that person who knows God has something for you, but you can't quite make out what it is. The vision is there, but it's a little fuzzy still.

Or maybe you're standing at your own crossroads right now, looking down different paths, trying to figure out which one's right. It's like being in a maze where one turn could change everything. I know how scary that feels.

God has a plan. That's the truth that changed everything for me.

Not just any plan, but a perfect plan, designed specifically for you. His plan is bigger than your dreams, better than your experience, and more purposeful than you can imagine. And He's not playing hide and seek with His plan for you—He wants you to discover it. He wants to direct your future.

Ephesians 2:10 says this clearly: "For we are God's handiwork, created in Christ Jesus to do good works, which God prepared in advance for us to do." (NIV).

Did you catch that? He prepared these works *in advance.* That means right now, this very minute, there are good works with your name on them, just waiting for you to step into them.

Psalm 37:23 puts it this way: "The steps of a [good and righteous] man are directed and established by the Lord, And he delights in his way [and blesses his path]" (AMP)

That's no small promise! When you're walking with God, He directs your steps and blesses your path.

God's plan is the perfect plan for you. He created you, after all, so He knows you better than anyone. He knows exactly what abilities and gifts He put in you, and His plan will allow you to use those things to the fullest.

That's why 1 Corinthians 7:17 says, "Only let each person lead the life that the Lord has assigned to him, and to which God has called him" (ESV). Notice that word "assigned." God doesn't just throw us out there to figure everything out on our own. He helps us "understand the assignment."

God's will for your life isn't some mass-produced, one-size-fits-all plan. He takes everything about you—your strengths, your weaknesses, even those things you think are mistakes—and weaves them into His purpose. You don't have to:

- Be afraid of what's coming.
- Live paralyzed by stress or anxiety.
- Wander around lost.
- Make big mistakes.
- Give up on finding your purpose.
- Settle for less than God's best.
- Figure this out alone.

Seek God's plan for you—for your career, your family, your ministry, your church, your relationships—and follow it with all your heart. He will lead you through every challenge and difficulty and take you into His perfect future.

ALYSSA'S STORY

Born and raised in a strong Christian home, I always believed that God had a plan for my life. I knew as I served Him faithfully throughout my high school years that God would direct me, as all I wanted was to pursue the call of God.

In grade 12 I was motivated by my junior high plan of being a doctor, so I registered for biological sciences at RDP as a pre-med, and I had a verbal commitment with the women's soccer team. I thought I had figured it out, as I had worked extremely hard to reach this point as a student and athlete.

However, when February of my grade senior year hit, I found myself dreading college. I suddenly felt unsettled about this version of my future that I had been planning for so long, so I started praying for clarity and direction.

A few weeks after this realization, my mom brought up a conversation she had with a client about engineering. This was a career I had never considered before, but my conversation with her sparked a desire to research it. I then found myself getting excited about all the possibilities this career offered, and at that moment I decided I wanted to try. Still not fully aware of what engineering entailed, I felt peace and joy about pursuing engineering that I never had with medicine; like God was giving me a green light.

However, I had missed all the college application deadlines, so I planned to take a gap year. I knew God had put engineering on my heart and I was ready to pursue this next step. About two weeks after the deadline, I got an email from the University of Calgary about an application extension, as I had an unfinished pre-med application from October.

This was the answer to all my prayers. In a season of discomfort about my future, God swiftly closed the medical door and so evidently opened this new one, all within a month. I immediately applied and got in a few days later. It was my top choice university. Shortly after, I received a significant scholarship. It truly was all a miracle.

Throughout this season of preparing for my future, I faithfully served God and cried out for help, and He did not fail! Reflection on this journey is undeniable evidence of how God redirected my heart to align with His purpose. That fall I began engineering school in

Calgary, and after much prayer that first year, chemical engineering became the clear choice for my major. All credit for this decision goes to the new desires that God put on my heart.

Tithing is a practice I have implemented since I was a child. I love to give. It has always been a non-negotiable part of my life and is something I do with great joy. It is a small way to show my overwhelming gratitude to God. As I served God throughout college, He continued to bless me financially with more scholarships that paid for four years of my engineering degree—another miracle of many that assured my place in engineering.

I truly love what I do and feel so much purpose and peace in this pursuit. I know that God has big things in store. I praise Him every day for redirecting my life when I thought I had it all together. As I finish the final year of my degree, I am beyond excited to continue to honour God through a fulfilling career that would not exist without His unwavering loyalty to my purpose. I will forever praise God for His provision over my life.

—Alyssa

SCRIPTURES ABOUT GOD'S GUIDANCE

Psalm 37:23 (NKJV)
"The steps of a good man are ordered by the Lord,
and He delights in his way."

Proverbs 3:5–6 (NIV)
"Trust in the LORD with all your heart
and lean not on your own understanding;
in all your ways submit to him,
and he will make your paths straight."

Psalm 32:8 (NIV)
"I will instruct you and teach you in the way you should go;
I will counsel you with my loving eye on you."

Isaiah 30:21 (NIV)
"Whether you turn to the right or to the left,
your ears will hear a voice behind you, saying,
'This is the way; walk in it.'"

James 1:5 (NIV)
"If any of you lacks wisdom, you should ask God,
who gives generously to all without finding fault,
and it will be given to you."

Psalm 119:105 (NKJV)
"Your word is a lamp to my feet
and a light to my path."

Isaiah 58:11 (NIV)
"The LORD will guide you always;
he will satisfy your needs in a sun-scorched land
and will strengthen your frame.
You will be like a well-watered garden,
like a spring whose waters never fail."

Jeremiah 29:13 (NKJV)
"And you will seek Me and find Me,
when you search for Me with all your heart."

TIPS TO DISCOVER GOD'S PLAN FOR YOUR LIFE

"My sheep hear My voice, and I know them, and they follow Me" (John 10:27 NKJV).

1. Read the Bible daily and seek the Lord, asking Him for direction.
2. Listen to God's voice and develop a listening ear to hear what He has to say. He will speak to you in visions, dreams, and prophetic words and through good counsel.
3. When you're at church, listen to the voice of God. While the pastor is speaking, ask the Lord for a practical application to the message.
4. Ask advice from leaders who you can trust and listen to what they have to say.
5. Lay aside all your presuppositions regarding hearing God's voice.
6. Be patient and keep practicing. Learning to hear God's voice is a skill that is learned.
7. When God speaks, take immediate action. Don't put obedience off until later.

These practical steps will help open your spiritual eyes and ears. You'll start seeing God's fingerprints all over your life.

Don't get ahead of God, but instead, focus on what you need to be doing today. God won't give you more direction when you're not walking in the direction that you already have. Start where you are, and take wise steps forward.

His plan will be good, acceptable, and perfect for you. "Good" means that His plan for you is the best plan. "Acceptable" means that you will be satisfied with His plan and it will be a good fit for you. And "perfect" means that it will be exactly what you need.

Life is not perfect, but God has a perfect plan. Life will have its ups and down, and you'll face some disappointments along the way. But God's perfect plan will guard and guide you along the way.

LEVI'S STORY

My name is Levi Mullen. I grew up in the church. My grandpa was the Founding Pastor of Home Church, and in 2009 he handed the church down to my dad. But it wasn't until I was 12 years old when I made the decision to dedicate my life to Jesus. I was baptised and filled with the Spirit and never looked back. This is my story about how God's perfect will has impacted my life.

One of the biggest questions that every young person is asked is, "What career path are you going to take?" I remember being halfway through my second year of Bible college, and I had to start making decisions on what I was going to do the next year. I felt pressured as I wanted my work to be purposeful, to be something I really loved, and most importantly to be what I was called by God to do.

As application deadlines for universities were getting close, I remember taking weeks where I would fast and pray that God would show me where I needed to go. I came to the conclusion that I would go into law—mostly because I had good grades and because there is good money in the profession.

As I was coming to that conclusion and finishing applications for schools. Pastor Cheryl Koop came to visit from Vancouver. Little did I know, Pastor Cheryl is also a career advisor. My parents begged me to take a test from her to see what career would fit me best. I was stubborn because I thought those tests were absolute bogus, and they would not be able to tell who I was or what talents I had from a series of questions.

Anyhow, I was basically forced to take this test by my parents, and it literally read me like a book. I was shocked at how well it described how I work and react to different scenarios, but mostly at the recommendations of work fields I could enter. On a scale of 1 to 100, 1 being "Do not enter this field, you will hate your life", and 100 being "This is the perfect scenario for you". I scored a 1 in law, and a 99 in productions and entertainment.

Pastor Cheryl said that seeing someone score in the 99th per-centile of any field of work was basically unheard of. It was clear from there I had to make a switch and go into a creative field. I believe God answered my prayers and gave me a clear direction of where I was supposed to go through Pastor Cheryl's test.

This then led me to having to find where I fit in the creative field. So I started looking at different universities and film schools, but I wasn't having any luck. There weren't courses that seemed like the right fit for me. I went back to prayer and asked that God would bring me the right opportunity.

About a week later I got offered an internship at Celebration Church in their creatives department. And after praying about it and talking with my family and people I trusted, I knew that this was God providing an opportunity for me to learn multiple aspects of the cre-ative field and how I could apply my work to building God's church. I learned how to design graphics, how to shoot and edit videos, and how to design and lead stage builds from an absolutely world class staff.

Since then, I have moved back home and am working as the social media director at Home Church. I absolutely love my job. I feel like I am doing something that is full of purpose, and I know that I am living in the will of God. Even through seasons of uncertainty, the Lord was always guiding me. His will is better than anything I could ever have dreamt of, and I am so excited to see where He takes me in the future.

—Levi

QUESTIONS FOR REFLECTION

1. Have I established a belief that God has a plan for my life?

2. Have I made the decision that God's plan will be my plan for life?

3. Have I heard God speak to me? What did He say about my future?

4. What roadblocks do I need to overcome to pursue God's plan? What habits do I need to form to hear God's voice and follow His will?

5. What's the "next step" that I need to take right now, even though I might not see the entire path ahead? What's holding me back from taking that step today?

NOTES

_____

_____

_____

_____

_____

_____

_____

_____

_____

_____

_____

_____

_____

_____

_____

_____

_____

_____

_____

CHOICE 2
IDENTITY

I am who God says I am.

MY STORY

I was born on January 11 in a small hospital in Saskatchewan. The doctor took one look at me and said, "It's a boy," and my parents said, "We're naming him Melvin Clarence Mullen." And with those words, my identity was recorded on my birth certificate. In those days, nobody debated it or questioned it. That was the world I grew up in, built on the assumption that God had made me with purpose, design, and intention.

I share that moment from my birth because it represents something foundational in my own understanding of identity: the belief that I was created by God *on* purpose and *with* purpose, and that He didn't make a mistake when He formed me. I don't have to question who I am or doubt whether I have a place in this world, just as God made me. Instead, I have to understand and believe what God says about me: not just my gender, but my value, my potential, and my gifts.

You have the choice to believe what God says about your identity. Long before society had an opinion about you, God had already spoken over you. He designed you, planned you, formed you, shaped you, and prepared you. He got the world ready for you, and He got you ready for the world.

THE FOUNDATION OF YOUR IDENTITY

Psalm 139 says, "For you created my inmost being; you knit me together in my mother's womb. I praise you because I am fearfully and wonderfully made; your works are wonderful; I know that full well" (verses 13-14 NIV). That means you were not random. You were not accidental. Your personality, the way you think, the way you see the world, the strengths you carry, the potential inside you—none of these things came from chance. They came from your Creator.

Today, young people face so much pressure to define themselves, reinvent themselves, or "discover their truth." But the greatest truth you'll ever discover is this: your identity doesn't start with you—it starts with God. When your identity is grounded in Him, you find clarity instead of confusion, confidence instead of striving, and peace instead of pressure.

The next time you look in the mirror, instead of picking apart what you see, remind yourself that God doesn't make mistakes! Every detail about you—your personality, your height, your eye colour, your natural gifts—was designed on purpose by your Creator. Even the things you're tempted to dislike about yourself were shaped by the Master Craftsman, who doesn't make mistakes.

When you start attacking your appearance or putting yourself down, remember these words: "I praise you because I am fearfully and wonderfully made; your works are wonderful." Stop criticizing how God made you and start thanking Him for His incredible work in forming you. Yes, take care of yourself and do what you can to be healthy—but stop being your own worst critic. Embrace the uniqueness God gave you and see yourself the way He sees you.

You were created by God. You are not the byproduct of evolution or some universal accident; you were made with intention and care. Maybe your parents were surprised by your arrival, but God wasn't. You were always in His heart and mind. Reject any idea that you are a mistake—you were formed with purpose and love.

It wasn't just your gender, body shape, or personality that were formed by God. Your entire life is beautiful to Him, and He sees the wonderful future He created for you long before it comes to pass.

Psalm 139 continues, "Your eyes saw my unformed body; all the days ordained for me were written in your book before one of them came to be" (verse 16 NIV). That means that before you were even conceived, God had a plan for your life. He marked you for a divine purpose, mapped out your days, and designed you with intentionality. And God doesn't make mistakes.

One of the lies the enemy tries to plant in young people's minds is that life came from a big bang theory or we evolved from monkeys—that we are just an accident of science. You'll hear people say things like, "I believe in science, therefore I believe in evolution." But here's the truth: both views require faith. It takes faith to believe everything came from a random explosion, and it takes faith to believe everything came from a Creator. And I believe science actually points towards design. Just look at the intricate details of creation, from the human body to the universe itself—it's hard to deny the work of a Designer. The enemy tries to erase identity by erasing the Creator behind it.

Maybe someone has even told you that you were a "mistake" or an "accident." That is a lie straight from the pit of hell. It contradicts the heart of God, who personally knit you together with intention. Look at Psalm 139 again: "How precious to me are your thoughts, God! How vast is the sum of them! Were I to count them, they would outnumber the grains of sand" (verses 17–18 NIV). God thought more about creating you than you can even imagine.

You were formed on purpose and with purpose by a loving God.

IDENTITY IN CHRIST

Your identity goes far deeper than your personality, your background, or even the details of how God originally designed you. When you become a follower of Jesus, you receive an entirely new identity—one that is found "in Christ." This is a reality that begins the moment you surrender your life to Jesus.

The Bible says, "If anyone is in Christ, the new creation has come: The old has gone, the new is here!" (2 Corinthians 5:17 NIV). That means you're not defined by your past, your mistakes, your failures, or the labels others put on you. The moment Jesus saves you, you become a new person. God gives you a new heart, a new nature, and a new future. He writes your name in the Book of Life. You belong to Him now.

You also receive new citizenship—you become a citizen of Heaven. Earth is no longer your final home. You're part of God's family, the Church, and you have brothers and sisters all around the world. You're no longer alone or overlooked; you're deeply connected to the Body of Christ.

Throughout Scripture, when God changed someone's identity, He often gave them a new name to match their new calling.

- Abram became Abraham.
- Sarai became Sarah.
- Jacob became Israel.
- Simon became Peter.
- Saul became Paul.

Those name changes weren't random—they declared who God said they were, not who they used to be. In the same way, God places a new identity over your life. You may still have the same face, same voice, and same body, but spiritually, you are not the same. You are a child of God, the righteousness of God in Christ, and someone set apart for divine purpose.

This identity should be the anchor you build your life on. When the world tries to define you—by your failures, your appearance, your likes and followers, your performance, your gender or sexuality, your friend group—your identity in Christ stands stronger. You are who He says you are.

Think of Joseph. As a teenager, God gave him a dream. It was a glimpse of who he really was and what his future would be. His brothers rejected him. His circumstances went up and down. But the identity God placed on him stayed constant. And in time, he lived it out.

Think of Jeremiah, too. Before he ever gave a prophecy or preached a sermon, before he had any influence, before he felt qualified, God said, "Before I formed you in the womb I knew you, before you were born I set you apart" (Jeremiah 1:5 NIV). His identity didn't come from his age, his experience, or his confidence. It came from God's calling.

The same is true for you. You were not an accident or an afterthought. You were not a random combination of cells. You were formed by God, chosen by God, loved by God, and called by God.

Identity in Christ means lifting your head and walking like someone who belongs to the King of Kings. It means rejecting the lies that say you're not enough, you're too broken, or you have no future. It means embracing the truth that you are God's masterpiece and that He has placed greatness inside you.

So embrace your identity in Christ. Let it shape the choices you make. Let it decide the dreams you chase and the way you see your future. Become the remarkable person God designed you to be—and live boldly, knowing that your true identity is found in Him alone.

SCRIPTURES ABOUT YOUR IDENTITY

You are a child of God — 1 John 3:1 (NIV)
"See what great love the Father has lavished on us, that we should be called children of God! And that is what we are!"

You are forgiven — Ephesians 1:7 (NIV)
"In him we have redemption through his blood, the forgiveness of sins, in accordance with the riches of God's grace."

You are redeemed — Galatians 3:13 (NIV)
"Christ redeemed us from the curse of the law by becoming a curse for us."

You are accepted — Romans 15:7 (NIV)
"Accept one another, then, just as Christ accepted you, in order to bring praise to God."

You are free — Galatians 5:1 (NIV)
"It is for freedom that Christ has set us free. Stand firm, then, and do not let yourselves be burdened again by a yoke of slavery."

You are a new creation — 2 Corinthians 5:17 (NIV)
"Therefore, if anyone is in Christ, the new creation has come: The old has gone, the new is here!"

You are unconditionally loved — Romans 8:38–39 (NIV)
"For I am convinced that neither death nor life, neither angels nor demons, neither the present nor the future, nor any powers... will be able to separate us from the love of God that is in Christ Jesus our Lord."

You are sealed with the Holy Spirit — Ephesians 1:13 (NIV)
"When you believed, you were marked in him with a seal, the promised Holy Spirit."

You are chosen — 1 Peter 2:9 (NIV)
"But you are a chosen people, a royal priesthood, a holy nation, God's special possession, that you may declare the praises of him who called you out of darkness into his wonderful light."

You are God's masterpiece — Ephesians 2:10 (NIV)
"For we are God's handiwork, created in Christ Jesus to do good works, which God prepared in advance for us to do."

You are called — 2 Timothy 1:9 (NIV)
"He has saved us and called us to a holy life—not because of anything we have done but because of his own purpose and grace."

You are strengthened by the Holy Spirit — Ephesians 3:16 (NIV)
"I pray that out of his glorious riches he may strengthen you with power through his Spirit in your inner being."

You are more than a conqueror — Romans 8:37 (NIV)
"No, in all these things we are more than conquerors through him who loved us."

You are never abandoned — Hebrews 13:5 (NIV)
"God has said, 'Never will I leave you; never will I forsake you.'"

LIVING YOUR IDENTITY IN CHRIST

Knowing who you are in Christ is powerful, but you have to live it. Identity must become a lifestyle or it won't last. When you start walking like the person God says you are, everything in your life begins to shift: your habits, your friendships, your confidence, your purpose, and even the way you speak to yourself.

Here are a few practical ways to live out your identity every day:

1. Speak God's Word over your life daily.

Your words shape your mindset, your mindset shapes your decisions, and your decisions determine the course of your life. So make sure to speak the truth God has already spoken over you. That truth is found in His Word. Say things like:

- "I am a child of God."
- "I am a new creation."
- "God has a purpose for me."
- "Nothing can separate me from His love."

Your identity grows each time you replace lies with truth. The enemy will always try to attack your worth and your purpose. But every time you choose to speak God's Word instead of repeating the lies of the devil, you reinforce who you really are.

2. Reject labels that don't come from God.

Some labels might have been spoken over you by teachers, parents, friends, enemies, or even by yourself—labels such as *not enough, too much, broken, stupid, weird, failure, unlovable,* or *mistake.* None of those labels belong to you because God didn't speak them over you, and they don't describe the person He created.

When a negative thought or label rises up, stop and ask: Does this line up with what God says about me? If not, throw it out immediately. Don't waste emotional energy trying to argue with these thoughts or prove them wrong—just replace them with God's labels. You are loved, accepted, called, wonderful, and strong.

This is especially important when things go wrong or you make a mistake. Those are the times when negative labels and language will fill your mind. But you are not defined by your worst moment or your biggest weakness. You are defined by the God who created you, redeemed you, and calls you His own.

3. Surround yourself with people who call out the best in you.

Identity is strengthened (or weakened) by the people you choose to walk with. If you hang out with friends who pull you into drama, gossip, compromise, addictions, insecurity, or distraction, it becomes harder to live confidently in who you are.

But when you choose friends who encourage your faith, challenge your character, celebrate your purpose, and speak life into you, your identity grows stronger and stronger. Don't walk alone, and don't walk with people who are trying to pull you in a different direction. Instead, build community with people pursuing Jesus and His calling, just like you.

4. Practise disciplines that shape your heart.

As we saw in an earlier chapter, spiritual disciplines are not rules—they are tools. They build the roots of your identity and turn your decisions into habits that will carry you the rest of your life.

Simple daily habits strengthen who you are in Christ:

- Read God's Word, even a few verses.
- Pray openly and honestly.
- Worship, even when you don't "feel spiritual."
- Serve others.
- Attend church and youth group.
- Be generous

These habits remind your heart of the truth: you belong to Jesus, and your life has meaning.

5. Step boldly into your calling, even when you feel unqualified.

Identity becomes real when you start living like the person God created you to be. God doesn't wait for you to feel ready. He calls you forward now.

Take small steps, like serving in your church, praying for a friend, encouraging someone who needs it, volunteering, or saying yes to opportunities that stretch you. Every act of obedience strengthens your identity. Every step of faith shapes your future. And every moment you choose courage over comfort, you grow into the person God designed you to become.

Living out your identity in Christ is not about perfection, but about direction. It's about choosing, day by day, to walk in the truth that you are loved, chosen, called, forgiven, and set apart. When you live from that place, confidence rises. Purpose awakens. And your life becomes a testimony of God's goodness.

CHARLENE'S STORY

My story begins with a classic tale as a Filipino immigrant's child. My mother came to Canada in the mid-nineties without my father. She was the primary pioneer who set our family on a path of a greater quality of life and eventually got the papers needed to bring not just my father but my grandmother to Canada.

Not long after they had my older brother Paul-Mauriel, they struggled with infertility for a few years before getting pregnant with me. Even then, my life was not guaranteed. The doctors put my mom on bed rest early in her pregnancy just to keep me alive.

When I was growing up, my parents both worked two full-time jobs, which left very little time to spend with my brother and me. My grandmother lived with us until I was about seven years old and played a key part in my early childhood development. However, when she moved out, I quickly became hyper-independent, as my brother at the age of eleven or twelve did not have the capacity to raise a seven-year-old.

Through all of this—my parents' sacrifices, our Filipino culture, and my own hyper-independence—my identity became rooted in what I could do, not in who I was. I didn't see myself first as a daughter, either to my parents or to God. As a teenager, I was well-loved by peers and known as a peacemaker. People relied on me as a defender and a safe place to land. But when betrayal came from the very friends I had chosen as family, I was devastated. I tried to keep the peace and hold relationships together, but one night a friend told me bluntly, "Charlene, you should change who you are because we're all sick of you."

That single moment shattered any sense of identity I had. Everything I thought I was—that reliable, safe place for others— was completely defined by people's opinions of me. No words of comfort from others could undo the damage. By the time I was heading into grade 11, I had decided that since "everyone was sick of me," I would reinvent myself. I made a plan: when rugby conditioning started in November/December, I would join the party scene, sleep around, and throw away the morals I once held.

But God was already at work. That same summer, my brother Paul had joined a community I knew nothing about—Home Church. On October 14, 2018, he invited our grandma to attend, and since he wanted to sit with his friends, he had me sit with her. I had no idea that moment would completely course-correct my life.

For the first time, I encountered God in a real way. I couldn't understand how strangers could love and care about me when I had done nothing to earn it. For my whole life, love had always felt conditional. It took about nine months of leaders and spiritual family members consistently showing me unconditional love before I realised I wanted to be part of this community.

The summer of 2019 marked a turning point. At the annual Summer Conference, I found my youth leader, Judah-ann, stacking what must have been 800 chairs, all while recovering from broken ribs from a car accident prior. She was serving wholeheartedly, submitted to God, and I realised: she wasn't doing it for recognition, but because she loved Jesus and loved people. Something switched in me. That's who I wanted to be known as too: someone who loves Jesus and loves people.

Since then, I've gone to Bible college and gone deeper into God's Word, allowing it to shape and transform me into the woman He always intended me to be—the one He saw and knit together in my mother's womb. God has healed broken places in me I didn't even know were fractured, and He continues to make me whole. His hand and favour are on my life—not because of what I do, but simply because I've accepted His salvation and adoption as a daughter of the highest King.

—Charlene

QUESTIONS FOR REFLECTION

1. Are there areas where you have been letting culture, social media, or other people define your identity instead of God's Word?

2. What part of Psalm 139 speaks most to you right now—being created, being known, or being planned for—and why?

3. Are there any labels you've believed about yourself that don't line up with what God says about you? Which ones do you need to replace with truth?

4. How does knowing you are a "new creation in Christ" change the way you see your past, your struggles, or your future?

5. Who in your life helps strengthen your identity in Christ, and who weakens it? What changes do you need to make to walk confidently in who God made you to be?

NOTES

_____

_____

_____

_____

_____

_____

_____

_____

_____

_____

_____

_____

_____

_____

_____

_____

_____

_____

CHOICE 3

OBEDIENCE

"Why do you call me, 'Lord, Lord,'
and do not do what I say?" (Luke 6:46 NIV)

MY STORY

A good friend of mine owned a fishing boat and invited me to a salmon fishing experience off the West Coast of beautiful British Columbia. I decided to invite my pastor, Mel Davis, to join me on this great fishing adventure.

Sitting on the boat, waiting for the fish to bite on the line, I turned to my pastor and asked him, "What are some of the greatest lessons you have learned in life?"

He replied, "My greatest lesson was learning to obey God and do His will. I learned this when I was a young pastor in Trail, British Columbia. My wife Bernie and I were pastoring and life was difficult. The people were not responding to our leadership, so I decided to resign. I called my pastor in Vancouver and gave him the news. He invited me to move to Vancouver and become youth pastor in a large church. The church was one of the largest churches in Canada, and I was excited. I really loved the city of Vancouver and was very pleased to become the youth pastor of that great church. I started taking action: I sold the house and all the furnishings. But as I was packing the car to move to Vancouver, the Lord spoke to me: "Mel, I did not give you permission to move to Vancouver."

Still sitting in the boat, waiting in vain for the fish to bite, I asked, "Pastor Davis, what did you do?"

"I unpacked the car, purchased another house, stayed in Trail, British Columbia, and did what God told me to do. That was truly the greatest lesson of my life. Years later, I moved to Vancouver in the perfect will and timing of God."

The fishing experience was great, as we both caught many fish, including two nineteen-pound salmon! However, the lesson on obedience was even more important.

Let me ask you: **What is the level of your obedience to God?** Is your obedience to God partial, selective, or absolute? Because your level of obedience to God makes all the difference in life.

1. Partial obedience

When facing the Philistine army, Saul was instructed to wait seven days for Samuel to arrive and offer sacrifices before battle. As the days passed and Samuel hadn't shown up, Saul's troops began deserting out of fear. Instead of continuing to wait as commanded, Saul took matters into his own hands. He offered the sacrifices himself—something only priests were authorised to do.

Just as he finished, Samuel arrived. Saul's excuse sounds reasonable at first: "When I saw that the men were scattering, and that you didn't come at the set time, and that the Philistines were assembling at Mikmash, I thought, 'Now the Philistines will come down against me at Gilgal, and I have not sought the Lord's favour.' So I felt compelled to offer the burnt offering" (1 Samuel 13:11–12 NIV).

But Samuel didn't buy his excuses. Instead, he replied: "You have done a foolish thing. You have not kept the command the Lord your God gave you... Now your kingdom will not endure" (verses 13–14). Saul's impatience and partial obedience cost him his kingdom.

Obedience is a matter of the heart, not just outward actions. As God said through the prophet Samuel, "To obey is better than sacrifice" (1 Samuel 15:22 NIV). We can obey begrudgingly, or we can choose to obey joyfully out of love and trust for God. Scripture shows us that God desires obedience from the heart. When our obedience flows from a heart surrendered to God, we position ourselves to receive His guidance, blessing, and abundant life.

2. Selective obedience

Years ago, we were having special prophetic ministry at the church. Individuals would come forward and receive a word of encouragement for their life. In the service that day was a lady who lived a very confused life. I thought if she received prayer and a word, it might help her to make some good decisions.

As she was leaving the service that morning, I said to her, "I welcome you to return to the service tonight and receive special prayer. Maybe the Lord will have a word for you. If the Lord spoke to you, would you do what His word encouraged you to do with your life?"

Her answer was, "Well, it would depend on what the Lord said to me."

We will live a confused and less-productive life if we choose selective obedience to the Word of God.

3. Absolute obedience

Absolute obedience is "Just doing what God says." Absolute obedience is not only hearing the Word of God but doing the Word of God.

When you commit to obeying God absolutely, it means you decide beforehand to do *what* He asks, *when* He asks you to do it, even if it's hard. You don't obey partially (which is really just disobedience). And you don't obey selectively, only when it's convenient or you agree. Instead, you settle in your heart that God's ways are the best, His Word is right, and His plans are perfect for you. You trust that even if what God says is hard to do or doesn't make sense now, in the long run, it's always the best way to go.

SCRIPTURES ABOUT OBEDIENCE

James 1:22-25 (NKJV)
But be doers of the word, and not hearers only, deceiving yourselves. For if anyone is a hearer of the word and not a doer, he is like a man observing his natural face in a mirror; for he observes himself, goes away, and immediately forgets what kind of man he was. But he who looks into the perfect law of liberty and continues in it, and is not a forgetful hearer but a doer of the work, this one will be blessed in what he does"

John 14:23 (NLT)
Jesus replied, "All who love me will do what I say. My Father will love them, and we will come and make our home with each of them."

John 15:10 (NLT)
When you obey my commandments, you remain in my love, just as I obey my Father's commandments and remain in his love.

Deuteronomy 11:26–28 (NLT)
"Look, today I am giving you the choice between a blessing and a curse! You will be blessed if you obey the commands of the Lord your God that I am giving you today. But you will be cursed if you reject them."

Romans 6:16 (NLT)

Don't you realise that you become the slave of whatever you choose to obey? You can be a slave to sin, which leads to death, or you can choose to obey God, which leads to righteous living.

Philippians 2:12–13 (NLT)

Dear friends, you always followed my instructions when I was with you. And now that I am away, it is even more important. Work hard to show the results of your salvation, obeying God with deep reverence and fear. For God is working in you, giving you the desire and the power to do what pleases him.

THE RPJ PRINCIPLE

The apostle Paul gave us a guide for living in obedience and alignment with God's kingdom in Romans 14:17: "For the kingdom of God is not eating and drinking, but righteousness and peace and joy in the Holy Spirit" (NKJV). I call this the RPJ principle.

Righteousness. This means choosing to do the right thing according to God's principles, even when it's hard. This builds spiritual strength.

Peace. When we obey God's leading, we experience an inner peace and certainty that we are on the right path.

Joy. Obedience ultimately leads to profound joy, which is deeper and more lasting than temporary pleasures or happiness.

As you face decisions in your day-to-day life, use the RPJ principle as an internal compass. Ask yourself: Is this choice righteous? Does it give me peace? Will I feel joy if I go this direction?

When you're with your friends, you can use the same compass. Ask: Are these relationships encouraging me to walk righteously, or are they leading me down a different path? Do we have peace and joy when we're together, or is there division, jealousy, strife, or hatred?

You can even use this principle as you evaluate your future. Will this career or college I'm considering help me promote righteousness, or will it be a snare for me? Do I sense God's peace about going this direction, or do I feel confusion or unrest? Will this lead to a life of godly joy, or to stress or anguish?

The RPJ principle doesn't mean life will always be easy. Righteousness is often the harder path to take in the moment, but it leads to better results. Godly peace and joy are deeper and more permanent than happy feelings, and you can experience them even when you're going through hard times.

God's kingdom is righteousness, peace, and joy in the Holy Spirit. If you allow God to lead you with this principle, you'll enjoy the rewards of His kingdom throughout your life.

PLANTING SEEDS OF OBEDIENCE

Our choices, whether towards obedience or disobedience, produce long-term fruit in our lives, just as a planted seed yields a harvest. As Paul wrote, "Do not be deceived: God cannot be mocked. A man reaps what he sows. Whoever sows to please their flesh, from the flesh will reap destruction; whoever sows to please the Spirit, from the Spirit will reap eternal life." (Galatians 6:7-8 NIV).

When we sow seeds of obedience to God's Spirit and His Word, we reap a wonderful harvest of blessing in our lives. The choice is ours—do we want to plant seeds that lead to life, fruitfulness, and peace, or seeds that lead to corruption?

Again, this passage is about lifestyles, not just a one-time choice. A life characterized by selfish choices will become corrupted. One that's characterized by God-focused choices will be secure. These results are the natural consequences of the lifestyles we choose. So, make good choices!

Remember that God is not vindictive or angry, lashing out at those who disobey. The point of obedience isn't to "not make God mad." Rather, it's to put yourself in the wise, safe, Christ-centred paths that God designed for you. God knows what is best for you and encourages you to follow those paths so that your life will be blessed.

Also, we don't earn God's blessing by our obedience. The word "blessing" refers to a gift we don't deserve. God is always good to us, even when we don't deserve it. Our obedience doesn't convince God to bless us. But it does keep us from wasting or ruining His blessings by making wrong choices.

Throughout your life, stay committed to God's will. Whether times are bad or times are good, listen to God. Whether you are facing challenges or experiencing victory, seek His will. Whether the road is hard or easy, follow Him. You won't regret it. His ways are always best.

Each one of us gets to choose what seeds we will plant through our choices. The paths of obedience and disobedience lead to vastly different destinations over time. Will you choose to sow to the Spirit by obeying God's voice, or will you sow to the desires of the flesh?

One path leads to a harvest of life, peace, and joy, while the other only reaps corruption over time. As Proverbs 4:18 says, "But the path of the just is like the shining sun, that shines ever brighter unto the perfect day" (NKJV). Each day, you choose your path.

THE SECRET POWER OF A CLEAR CONSCIENCE

Life is not easy to figure out at times. Sometimes you'll face questions that don't have clear answers, or you'll make a choice and then wonder afterward if it was the right one. As you navigate these tricky decisions, learn to listen to your conscience.

The conscience is the inner light that God has placed in every person. From a young age, we know that right and wrong exist, and we have a sense that what helps people is good while what harms them is bad. As we grow, our parents, teachers, society, and other voices help us learn the difference between right and wrong. The Bible, of course, is the best source of information about right and wrong, and it helps train our conscience and understand whether our actions or choices are the right ones. Sin, on the other hand, weakens or dulls our conscience.

Having a clear conscience is an important key to life. There are few things as miserable as a guilty conscience, and few things as freeing as a clean, clear conscience. God will often speak to us through our conscience to show us how we are doing or whether there are areas that need to change. That inner voice brings conviction of sin and nudges us to repent and make things right.

A few years ago, as I got older, I began to lose some of my hearing abilities. I didn't recognise what was going on at first because the changes were gradual. All I knew was that my wife talked too quietly, the TV was never loud enough, and people mumbled a lot. Social interactions were often embarrassing because I would misunderstand what people were saying, so I would sometimes take the conversation in a completely different direction. When I figured out what was happening, I went to a hearing specialist and purchased much-needed hearing aids. Suddenly, life became a lot better because I could hear again.

Just as I needed to hear the voices of those around me clearly through hearing aids, we need to be able to hear God's voice of guidance if we are to obey it. God is speaking all the time, but if we're not paying attention, we can be like the people described in Hebrews: "spiritually dull and don't seem to listen" (5:11 NLT).

If you need wisdom and direction, Scripture promises that when you ask God, "He will not rebuke you for asking" (James 1:5 NLT). He happily guides and protects those willing to listen and obey.

PRACTICAL WAYS TO HEAR GOD'S VOICE

1. **Preparation**: Read and meditate on Scripture daily to renew your mind.

2. **Surrender**: Lay down your own desires and ask God to align your will with His.

3. **Listen**: Find a quiet place to pray and listen for His still, small voice.

4. **Patience**: Be patient and persistent - hearing takes practice.

5. **Confirmation**: Check that the voice lines up with Scripture and godly counsel.

6. **Obedience**: Obey whatever He tells you, even if it's difficult.

As you become more sensitive to God's voice through these steps, His guidance will become increasingly clear. He delights in leading those who are willing to follow wherever He goes.

The choice to obey God may not always be easy, but it is always worth it. His ways lead to life, blessing, peace, and joy that this world can never give you. God has promised that those who are willing and obedient will eat the good of the land (Isaiah 1:19).

So, the question is this: Will you trust Him enough to do what He says, even when you don't completely understand it? Will you obey him even when personal sacrifice is required? Step out in bold obedience, and you will find that God is faithful to guide your steps into the wonderful future He has planned.

TIDA'S STORY

Hi my name is Tida. I was born and raised in Japan. I came to faith in Christ through my grandmother who was a pastor in a small house church. There weren't many of us, but it made it feel like we were all family. Everything I believed about God, Christianity, and the church was strongly rooted in what my grandmother believed, so when she passed away in 2019, my faith fell apart. For a while, I wandered, not knowing how or where to search for another church I could call home. It was around this time I also needed to make crucial decisions about my future. Not wanting to go into post-sec-ondary education, unlike a large majority of my peers, I decided to pursue the idea of attending a Bible college in Canada to become more rooted in my faith. And so I came to Canada in 2020 for a fresh start. Oddly enough, the first time I attended a Sunday service, I felt like "I was back."

After two years of Bible College, I felt more rooted in my faith, having met godly friends, mentors, and even been welcomed into families. Having people alongside you that are also striving to be like Jesus profoundly impacts your walk as a Christian.

However, this is where the story takes a turn. After completing Bible college, I had no purpose. I was among strong believers but felt lost. I travelled back to Japan to visit family. What I had planned to be a three-week visit turned into a seven-month stay, filled with depression and confusion. I fell back into old patterns of sin and distanced myself from God. I had truly lost sight of how to live a purpose-filled life. Looking back, I realise that God was calling to me all along, but I refused to listen because I felt unworthy. One night as I was lying on my bed, I heard the voice of God so clearly say to me: "Get out of bed and start repenting." Without skipping a beat, I rolled out of bed, got on my knees, and started to repent. God told me in that moment that He was not done with me and that He wanted me to return to Canada. Logically, this made no sense. I had no blood relatives there, no career, and no future goals. But the Holy Spirit led me to take a step of obedience and move back to Canada. God gave me a second chance, and I had to make a decision and fully commit to following His plan and will. I honestly don't know where I would be if I didn't make that conscious choice to answer God's call. It has been over three years since I returned, and I feel driven to build and serve in God's church like never before. I encourage you to obey God when He calls you because the plan and purpose He has for your life is far greater than the one you have.

—Tida

QUESTIONS FOR REFLECTION

1. Have you made Jesus the Lord of your life? When did you make that decision?

2. What was the level of your obedience to God in the past: partial, selective, or absolute? What level of obedience will you have going forward?

3. In what areas are you currently struggling to choose obedience to God's Word and His ways?

4. Hearing God's voice clearly is key to obeying His guidance. Which of the six practical steps listed for hearing God's voice do you need to implement more faithfully in your life right now? What could help make that a priority?

NOTES

CHOICE 4

FRIENDS

"Bad company ruins good morals." (1 Corinthians 15:33 ESV)

MY STORY

I was nineteen years old and attending my first year of Bible college. I was a sincere follower of Jesus who was seeking God's perfect will for my life. I practiced daily prayer and Bible reading along with attending my Bible classes. One morning when I began to pray, I saw an image in my head of my childhood go-kart.

Growing up in Southern Saskatchewan, every young lad built a go-kart, and we would race down the hills and valleys. It was so much fun. One day the wheel on the front of the go-kart seized when the bearing gave in to the pressure, and my go-kart quickly came to a stop.

My friend said to me, "Let's go to the used car parts store. I know where we can get a bearing for your go-kart."

We arrived at the store. It was a Saturday, so the shop was closed, and the fence had a lock on it. Looking over the fence, my friend saw a starter used in an automobile that he said would have the right part for the go-kart.

"Come on," he told me. "Let's climb over the fence and get that starter. We can take it apart, and we'll have everything you need to go racing again."

So we both climbed the fence, stole the starter, returned to his house, fixed the go-kart, and went racing again.

In Bible college, that memory came back to me. Every time I began to pray I had the same experience: I saw a picture of the starter and the stolen bearing. It seemed my relationship with God was blocked. I was so bothered about this sin from my childhood that I said, "Dear Jesus, please forgive me for this sin. I promise you that when I return home for Christmas, I will find the owner of the business, pay him for the starter, and ask him to forgive me."

When I asked God to forgive me, my relationship with God was restored. Then, when I returned to my home at Christmas, I did what I promised the Lord I would do. I found the owner of the business, told him my story, asked him to forgive me, and gave him the money. The owner of the business thanked me for my honesty, and I walked out of the business with a clean conscience. I was right with God and man.

I learned two principles from this experience. First, I learned you must ask God to forgive you for your sins *and* be in right relationship with people, including practicing restitution when needed. Forgiveness and resolution are so important in the life of every young adult. Second, I learned that I must surround myself with friends who have the highest level of honesty and who live with integrity. Obviously my friend's family had a different set of values than I had been raised to hold.

The questions I might ask you are: **Are you living with a clean conscience? Do you have friends who influence your integrity for good, or for evil? Are you living an honest life? Are you living with a clear conscience, or do you have a darkened conscience?**

WRONG FRIENDS CAN RUIN EVERYTHING

Friendships are so important in our lives because often they determine our future direction. In 2 Samuel 13, Amnon, King

David's firstborn son, became obsessed and so consumed with lust for his sister Tamar he made himself sick.

Jonadab, Amnon's friend and cousin, who the Bible describes as "a very crafty friend," gave him counsel: "I'll tell you what to do. Go back to bed and pretend you are ill. When your father comes to see you, ask him to let Tamar come and prepare some food for you" (verses 3–5 NLT).

Amnon followed this wicked advice, trapped Tamar in his room, and raped her. The devastation didn't stop there. Tamar's brother Absalom, enraged by what happened to his sister, plotted for two full years before murdering Amnon in revenge. This triggered a chain of events that led to Absalom's rebellion against David, civil war in Israel, and ultimately Absalom's own violent death.

Think about it—one evil friend's counsel led to rape, murder, rebellion, civil war, and the fracturing of David's entire kingdom. Multiple lives destroyed. A family torn apart. A nation divided. All because one young man chose to listen to the wrong voice at a crucial moment.

The friends you choose and the voices you listen to can either lead you towards God's best or towards destruction. There's no middle ground.

Simply put, your friends will shape your destiny. The Bible says, "Walk with the wise and become wise, for a companion of fools suffers harm" (Proverbs 13:20 NIV).

I've watched young people destroy their futures by choosing the wrong friends. I've also seen others soar beyond their dreams because they surrounded themselves with godly influences. This isn't just good advice. It's a spiritual principle that will determine your future.

Jesus modelled this principle perfectly. While He ministered to multitudes, He chose twelve disciples to pour His life into. Among the twelve, He had an inner circle of three: Peter, James, and John. These three witnessed things the others didn't. They saw the transfiguration. They were present in Gethsemane. They were there when He raised Jairus's daughter from the dead. When Jesus needed support in His darkest hour, He took these three with Him to pray. Even the Son of God knew He needed close friends who understood His mission and shared His values.

Years ago, one of our youth leaders would speak in high schools and repeatedly tell students something profound: "Show me your friends, and I'll show you your future." He was right. The people closest to you will either pull you up or drag you down. There's no middle ground. Your friends' values will become your values. Their habits will become your habits. Their dreams, or lack of dreams, will shape your aspirations.

AJ'S STORY

Hi, my name is AJ Ward. I was raised in a Christian family. I got saved at 11 and baptized at 13. For a few years I was mediocre, then at the age of 17, I got serious about following Jesus, and I had to make an important decision about who my friends were going to be. My friends were influencing me to do the wrong things, like partying and other things like that. I had to walk away from my old friends. I decided to go to Bible college and made new friends there, and it was the best decision I have made. They would influence me to do better and become closer to Jesus. One of the best things you can do is make sure your friends share the same beliefs as you. If they don't, instead of you influencing them, they will influence you.

—AJ

SCRIPTURES ABOUT FRIENDSHIP

Proverbs 13:20 (NLT)
"Walk with the wise and become wise; associate with fools and get in trouble."

1 Corinthians 15:33 (NLT)
"Don't be fooled by those who say such things, for 'bad company corrupts good character.'"

Proverbs 27:17 (NLT)
"As iron sharpens iron, so a friend sharpens a friend."

Proverbs 12:26 (NKJV)
"The righteous should choose his friends carefully, for the way of the wicked leads them astray."

Psalm 1:1 (NLT)
"Oh, the joys of those who do not follow the advice of the wicked, or stand around with sinners, or join in with mockers."

Proverbs 22:24–25 (NLT)
"Don't befriend angry people or associate with hot-tempered people, or you will learn to be like them and endanger your soul."

Hebrews 10:24–25 (NLT)
"Let us think of ways to motivate one another to acts of love and good works... encouraging one another."

WHAT VOICES ARE YOU LISTENING TO?

When my children, Jachin and Christy, were growing up, I gave them a clear rule: "You can make all the decisions you want, as long as they're the right decisions. But when you start making wrong decisions, I'll start making your decision for you. As long as you're living under our roof and eating at our table, you'll have to have the right friends." This wasn't about control—it was about protection. I knew their friends would either strengthen their walk with God or pull them away.

We're living in times when the world desperately wants to separate you from good parental influence. It pushes you to make "independent" decisions before you're ready. But here's what you need to understand: the enemy is strategic. He knows if he can isolate you from godly counsel, he can derail your future. That's why he makes peer pressure so powerful. That's why he paints rebellion as freedom. That's why he whispers that your parents are out of touch and don't understand.

I hear people say, "Well, teenagers need to learn things the hard way." That's not wisdom, that's foolishness. Why should loving parents suddenly stop protecting their children just because they turned thirteen? Your parents aren't trying to control your life; they're trying to protect you from the enemy's carefully laid traps. And often those traps come wearing the face of a friend.

The people you spend the most time with will have the greatest influence on you, which means you need to make sure you choose your close friends wisely. This doesn't mean you never spend time with people who have different values, though. Jesus himself was called a friend of tax collectors and sinners. He reached out to everyone. But while Jesus loved everyone, He didn't let everyone influence Him. He knew the difference between reaching out and being pulled in. He never compromised His values. He never adjusted His standards. He influenced them; they didn't influence Him.

Jesus had distinct circles of relationship. First, He had the crowds who followed Him. Thousands of people came to hear Him teach and receive healing. Second, He had the seventy He sent out to minister. Third, He had the twelve disciples He lived with, taught, and trained. And finally, He had the three He trusted most: Peter, James, and John. Not everyone had the same access to His life.

You need this same pattern. Some people will be *acquaintances* you're friendly with but don't spend much time around. Some will be *friends*, or people you enjoy being with and sharing activities with. But only a few *covenant friends* should be close enough to influence your major life decisions. These are the ones who will shape your future.

COVENANT FRIENDSHIPS

Let me tell you what to look for in these closest friends. First, they need to be faithful people. I met Akihiro Mizuno in Bible College when we were both young men. He was from Japan, I was from Canada, but God knit our hearts together. For over fifty years now, despite living in different countries, we've stayed connected. That's covenant friendship. These aren't casual relationships that fade when life gets hard. These are the friends who stick closer than a brother.

Second, they must be godly. Jesus said, "You are my friends if you do what I command" (John 15:14 NIV). Don't be fooled by someone who just talks about faith. Look at their life. Do they follow Christ when it costs them something? Do they stand for truth when everyone else compromises? These friends will strengthen your walk with God, not weaken it.

Third, they must be trustworthy. I'm talking about people who will tell you the truth even when it hurts. People who can keep confidence. People who won't smile to your face and destroy you behind your back. If a person cannot be trusted to keep confidences, don't trust them with your friendship.

Fourth, they need to complement your strengths and weaknesses. None of us has it all together. You need friends who are strong where you're weak. Friends who know more than you in areas where you need to grow. Friends who will challenge you to be better.

One of the best examples in the Bible of covenant friendship is the story of David and Jonathan. They met after David killed Goliath and won a victory against the Philistines. The Bible says that "Jonathan became one in spirit with David, and he loved him as himself" (1 Samuel 18:1 NIV).

Jonathan made a pact with David, promising loyalty and saying that he loved him as his own soul (1 Samuel 20:17). He even gave David his robe, armour, sword, bow, and belt as a symbol of their brotherly love (1 Samuel 18:4). Though David was anointed to one day replace Jonathan's own father as king, Jonathan willingly took second place, putting his friend's success before his own interests.

Over the following years, Jonathan proved himself a true covenant friend time and again. When King Saul sought to kill David out of jealousy, Jonathan risked his own life to warn and protect his friend.

Tragically, their friendship was cut short when Jonathan was killed in battle alongside his father Saul. David was overcome with grief. Their story shows the life-changing impact of choosing godly, covenant friendships.

THE ULTIMATE COVENANT FRIENDSHIP

These principles of covenant friendship lead to the most important relationship decision you'll ever make—choosing your life partner. This is a covenant that will shape your destiny, your calling, and every area of your life. The person you marry will either magnify your God-given purpose or derail it. There's no middle ground.

Let me be clear about something. Dating isn't just about finding someone to spend time with or someone who makes you feel good. It's about finding the person God has chosen to help you fulfil His purpose for your life. This decision is too important to leave to feelings, chance, or the world's standards. You need God's wisdom. You need His timing. You need His choice.

Proverbs 18:22 (NLT) tells us, "The man who finds a wife finds a treasure, and he receives favour from the LORD." Marriage is more than just a relationship. It's a covenant partnership between a man and a woman for life.

For me that covenant relationship started on a Bible college campus when a pretty student named Heather walked by. As I looked at her with admiration, I heard a still small voice inside my mind and heart say, *She is the one*. I knew it was God speaking. Heather would be my partner for life, and I knew right then I was to pursue her.

Interestingly, I had known her for many years, never once thinking she would be my life partner until that day I heard God's voice. Heather was stunning: a wonderful Christian leader, committed to the church, gifted in music, and skilled as a teacher. Later, I discovered she had a strong calling to carry the gospel to other nations. Together we would plant a great church that now reaches nations, and we would travel the world. But more than that, we would enjoy life together and live it to the fullest.

Too many young people make the wrong decisions and marry outside of God's will for their lives. They end up facing the consequences of that wrong decision. Just look at the statistics! I've read that over 60% of marriages in both the United States and Canada end in divorce. Think about that for a minute. Aren't those risks too high to make a mistake?

When a newly married young person asks me what they should do if they discover they made the wrong choice, the answer is simple. Because they said, "I do and I will, for better or for worse," my counsel is always this: "Make it work. With God's help, you can build a successful marriage and family, asking God for His grace."

Standing at that altar, those sacred words have deep significance and should not be taken lightly: "Will you take _____ to be your lawfully wedded spouse, for better or for worse, in sickness and in health, to love and to cherish, until death do us part?" When I spoke those words to Heather, I meant every single one.

Recently, I was in the elevator of a huge hotel in a leading city in the USA. A young couple stepped in, and he was smiling from ear to ear. I asked how they were doing, and he said they'd just gotten married yesterday.

I said, "Congratulations. Marriage is for life. I've been married for fifty-five years."

His wife spoke up and said, "I'm just hoping it works." She didn't seem nearly as happy about their first night as he was.

I hope it works too, but I have my doubts!

Marriage is serious business—it's taking a person for *life*. It's the second most important decision you'll ever make, right after making Jesus the Lord of your life.

Let's look again at Proverbs 18:22 (NIV). "The man who finds a wife finds a treasure, and he receives favour from the Lord." Notice the word *finds*. Scripture shows us you must search for the right person.

Think about the story in Genesis 24 of Abraham sending his servant Eliezer to find a wife for his son Isaac. Abraham is a picture of Father God, and Eliezer represents the Holy Spirit. Abraham sent

Eliezer to a distant land to find someone who had the same beliefs and values, someone who would be the right match for Isaac. The future of the nation of Israel depended on Eliezer finding the right person for Isaac.

Finding the right person for you isn't something that happens by accident. God has the right person in mind for you, and He knows the right time for you to find each other. Set a goal to find the kind of person you want, from the right family background, who has the same beliefs as you, and whose calling in life will set the stage for generations to come. That's why marriage is a serious decision that can't be taken lightly.

There's something worse than being single, and that's marrying the wrong person. So how do you know if you're marrying the right person? Here are some questions to ask.

1. Who is God's choice for your life?

Just like God spoke to me about Heather that day on campus, He wants to direct your path in this crucial decision. When I counsel young people, I often ask them, "Have you spent as much time praying about this person as you have dating them?" God's choice for your life will enhance your calling, not compete with it.

2. Is it God's timing?

I've watched too many young people rush into relationships because they're afraid of being alone or because "everyone else is dating." Don't fall into that trap. God's timing is perfect, and His timing is worth waiting for. There's no need to rush into multiple dating relationships as that just creates soul ties and emotional baggage you'll have to deal with later. Why waste precious years of your youth on relationships that aren't going anywhere when you could be developing your gifts, pursuing your education, or serving in ministry?

3.   Are you spiritually, emotionally, and financially prepared?

This is about being mature enough to build a life together. Seek God and know His will before pursuing any relationship. Too many young couples jump into marriage before they are ready, then spend their first years struggling because they didn't prepare properly.

You need more than love to build a life together—you need wisdom. How will you support your family? What's your plan for education, for housing, for the future? I'm not saying you need to be wealthy to get married, but you do need to think things through. So many marriages are strained because couples didn't talk about money until after the wedding.

Get godly counsel and not just from friends your age, but from spiritual leaders who can see what you might miss. What are they saying about your choices? Are you listening?

4.   Have you established boundaries and committed to purity?

This is about protecting your future marriage. Write down clear guidelines: How often will you see each other? What are your standards for purity? Where are your physical boundaries? So many couples have to deal with the consequences of rushing into physical intimacy. When you make a covenant commitment to purity, you're making a promise to each other as well as to God. That covenant will protect your relationship and set a foundation for your future marriage.

5.   Are you asking the right questions?

Do your gifts, calling, and life direction align? That means you have similar calls from God, interchangeable goals in life, and common priorities and commitments. When young people ask me about who they should marry, I always point them back to purpose: "Discover your purpose in life first. Then find someone who shares that purpose."

6.   Do you have the parents' blessing?

This isn't just some old-fashioned tradition; it's biblical wisdom. I've watched young couples struggle for years because they ignored their parents' concerns. Getting that parental blessing isn't just a formality. It's a covering of protection and wisdom over your future marriage. When parents who love God have serious reservations, that's a red flag you can't afford to ignore.

7.   Do you have an accountability "safety net"?

Couples who have strong accountability usually have strong marriages. Don't just choose one person, but instead build a network of accountability. Find people who will ask you the hard questions instead of just telling you what you want to hear. When Heather and I were dating, we had people in our lives who kept us on track and who weren't afraid to speak truth when we needed to hear it.

8.   Are you truly compatible?

This goes deeper than just enjoying the same movies or music. Are you spiritually compatible? Emotionally compatible? Do you share the same values about family, about ministry, about life? Are your personalities compatible? While we often marry someone whose personality, traits, or style complements ours through diversity, we cannot be so different that daily life becomes a struggle for unity.

Before you marry, you need to ensure that your future spouse is committed to Jesus, His Word, His Church, and His people, as well as being totally committed to you. The people you surround yourself with and the person you marry will shape your destiny more than almost any other decisions you make. These aren't just social choices—they're spiritual decisions that will affect generations to come.

For your friendships, remember the pattern Jesus showed us. Have a clear inner circle of covenant friends who share your values, strengthen your faith, and support your God-given purpose. Be intentional about who gets close enough to influence your life decisions. Don't let guilt, pressure, or fear of loneliness keep you in relationships that pull you away from God's best.

For your future marriage, don't settle for less than God's choice. More than just finding someone who makes you happy, find someone who will help you fulfil God's purpose for your life.

Remember what we discussed about God's timing. He's not going to bring your life partner too early or too late. He'll bring them at exactly the right time—when you're ready, when they're ready, and when His purpose for both of you is ready to be fulfilled.

Until then, focus on becoming the right person rather than finding the right person. Take time to develop yourself spiritually. Learn to hear God's voice clearly. Deal with your own issues before you try to build a life with someone else.

If you need to make changes in your relationships, do it now. Not next week. Not next year. Now. You might need to lovingly distance yourself from some friends. You might need to end a dating relationship that isn't God's will. You might need to have some difficult conversations. Whatever it takes, choose now to align your relationships with God's purpose for your life.

Your future is too important to leave to chance. Your destiny is too precious to risk with the wrong relationships. Every friendship choice you make today, every dating decision you make right now, is shaping your tomorrow. Choose wisely, for in choosing your relationships, you're choosing your future.

AMINA'S STORY
Kazakhstan

My name is Amina. I was born into a Christian family, and at the age of 16, I accepted Jesus. Before I was saved, I always thought that God didn't love me. Hearing different stories of salvation, I often felt like I wasn't special for being born into a Christian family. I thought, "God only loves sinners," since I was trying to live a "saintly" life. But I didn't realise that simply being born into a Christian family is not enough to receive salvation.

At 14, I lost all of my friends. In that moment, I started to believe even more that God didn't love me—that He had taken away everything I held dear. Later, things became even harder. My family started going through major problems, and that crushed me even more on the inside. I tried to find at least some kind of joy in the world to fill the emptiness inside me, but nothing ever satisfied me fully. Instead, it only hurt me more.

One day, I heard a very serious heresy that was related to God's word. Even though I wasn't reading the Bible at that time, I had often heard about it from other believers. But this time, what I heard sounded so strange and confusing. I thought, "I've never heard anything like this before." Then a question came to my mind: "Is this really true...?" That question wouldn't leave me, so I decided to search for the answer myself. I started reading the Bible we had at home. I made a decision that even if I didn't understand everything, I would keep reading, because I truly wanted to find the truth. And I did.

While reading God's Word in search of an answer to my question, I found salvation in Jesus' redemption for my sins. That was the moment when I was able to repent before God and finally feel His love. I realised what the Lord had done for me, and the lie I had believed for so many years melted away in Jesus and the love He showed by dying on the cross. 1 John 4:9: "God showed how much he loved us by sending his one and only Son into the world so that we might have eternal life through him" (NLT).

It became clear to me that God had never been demanding holiness from me. Instead, He had already prepared the perfect way to holiness through His Son, so that we could be holy in Him and with Him!

From that moment on, my life began to change in a wonderful way. God brought believing people into my life, and that was the time when He healed the wound of losing my friends by giving me new ones! Through them, God changed my perspective on friendship. They went through difficulties with me—even in moments when I completely ignored them in times of great depression, they kept praying and trying to reach my heart.

I didn't do anything to deserve such treatment, but God, through them, showed me His boundless love. And through that love, I also learned how to love just like He does. Through my friends, I also came to understand that friendship isn't just about spending time together and helping each other—it's also about being an example. An example of Jesus in the life of every person who has Him inside.

From them, I can learn new things, just as they can learn from me. The Body of Christ is an essential part of our faith that brings us even closer to Christ, and I'm so thankful to be a part of it.

—Amina

QUESTIONS FOR REFLECTION

1. Are you living with a clear conscience?

2. Who are the five most important people in your life right now, and are they friends you can trust?

3. Are you surrounding yourself with dream-builders or dream-killers?

4. Who needs to be added to your inner circle?

5. Does each of your relationships contribute to your best future?

NOTES

_____

_____

_____

_____

_____

_____

_____

_____

_____

_____

_____

_____

_____

_____

_____

_____

_____

_____

_____

_____

_____

FRIENDS

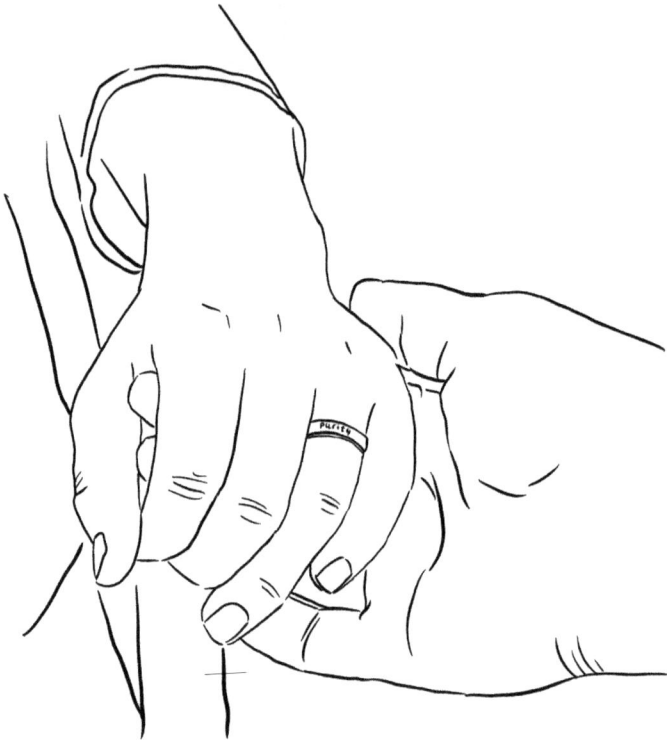

CHOICE 5

PURITY

"Keep yourself pure" (1 Timothy 5:22 NKJV).

MY STORY

It was late in the evening, and Heather and I were to witness a beautiful ceremony and a pledge for purity.

Our granddaughter Ava had turned 13, and Jachin (my son) had purchased a beautiful ring in Hawaii and was about to place the ring on Ava's finger, establishing a covenant of purity until marriage. Ava was committed to living in purity and abstaining from sexual intimacy with anyone until God directed her future in marriage. It was a promise she was making to God, witnessed by family members and some of her closest friends.

I will not forget the moment when Jachin and Becca placed the ring on Ava's finger, words were spoken, and the commitment to live in purity was made. She was surrounded by family and friends, and after the ring was given, each person said words of affirmation.

I remember the words of her cousin Jade who said, "Ava, I am so proud of you for making this covenant today. This is one of the best decisions you will ever make. My advice is to set a standard for your life and stay grounded in your beliefs, always influencing others with your faith. Never allow society's standards to define yours."

At the end of the ceremony, we held a time of prayer which established the covenant of purity and a commitment to God.

If you are a young person, why not make the same commitment today, even if in the past you haven't lived in purity? And if you are a parent or a grandparent, why not establish this principle with your children or grandchildren, leading them into a covenant relationship with God to live a morally pure life? As Jade said, it's one of the best decisions you'll ever make.

WHAT IS PURITY?

Purity means being free from anything that contaminates or pollutes. It refers to something that is 100% authentic and true to its essence, unmixed with any impurities. Pure water doesn't contain dirt or chemicals that could cause illness. Pure air has no pollution. Pure gold has no other metals mixed into it.

Purity, therefore, speaks of wholeness, completeness, and integrity. To be pure is to be true to your authentic self—the person God created you to be. It means having undivided motives and an unstained character. Living in purity is less about avoiding sin and more about whole-heartedly pursuing and protecting the virtue, beauty, and moral integrity that God has placed within you.

True purity involves:

- Having a heart motivated by love and peace, not fear or bitterness.
- Having a mind focused on what is good, wholesome, and virtuous.
- Handling money and resources with integrity and generosity, not greed.
- Embracing God's design for sexuality, not following selfish lust.

Even outside the church, in a world full of contamination, moral compromise, and selfish excess, people naturally recognise and value moral purity. There is a longing in the human heart for what is authentic and undefiled, and there is something attractive and inspiring about individuals who live with integrity and a pure lifestyle.

I witnessed this truth firsthand many years ago when Home Church sent a team of young people to the Philippines from Canada, with a message "Free at Last," promoting a life of moral purity and freedom from addiction. When the team arrived in the Philippines, they were treated like visiting celebrities. The local press had gotten wind of their visit and mission, and the team was soon invited to visit the mayor's office and to share their story on national television. This message was loud and clear: "You can be free from drugs and live a life of purity when you accept Jesus Christ as your Lord and Saviour." Several thousand came to Christ on the Philippines tour.

No matter where we live, we each face countless temptations that can easily lure us off the path of purity through appealing yet fleeting pleasures. However, whenever we surrender to those temptations, we don't find lasting satisfaction. Instead, we end up losing precious things that cannot be replaced—peace of mind, self-respect, key relationships, our reputations, our health, or even our lives. Moral impurity always fails to deliver on its promises, while purity helps us flourish.

HOW TO LIVE IN PURITY

We must not lose sight of the value of moral purity. Romans 6:16 says, "Don't you realise that you become the slave of whatever you choose to obey? You can be a slave to sin, which leads to death, or you can choose to obey God, which leads to righteous living" (NLT).

Paul was saying that sin will always enslave us, with the goal to destroy us. But he goes on in verses 17–18 to add, "Thank God! Once you were slaves of sin, but now you wholeheartedly obey this teaching we have given you. Now you are free from your slavery to sin, and you have become slaves to righteous living."

We are free to select which path we take. That is the power of choice. While the path of moral purity is challenging, it is possible to walk in it successfully. Let me share some suggestions.

1. Ask God for help.

This is the most fundamental step—asking God for His help, wisdom, and grace to live in purity. Life isn't a harsh, pass/fail test, but a journey with a loving Father who desires to strengthen you. When you're feeling weak or tempted, pour out your heart to Him. He will faithfully provide the power you need to endure.

"The temptations in your life are no different from what others experience. And God is faithful. He will not allow the temptation to be more than you can stand. When you are tempted, he will show you a way out so that you can endure" (1 Corinthians 10:13 NLT).

2. Make a covenant with God.

Purity comes from a real covenant relationship with God based on His love and grace, not just behavioural changes. While you can't promise God perfection, you can make a solemn commitment to always pursue faithfulness with integrity, just as Job did: "I made a covenant with my eyes not to look with lust at a young woman" (Job 31:1 NLT). Small decisions to honour this covenant build lifelong patterns of self-discipline.

3.   Guard your mind.

Wrong actions are always preceded by wrong thoughts and beliefs that have taken root. Evaluate whether your recurring thought patterns align with truth and produce life, or come from wrong motivations. Then replace wrong mindsets by meditating on what is excellent, praiseworthy, and pure.

"And now, dear brothers and sisters, one final thing. Fix your thoughts on what is true, and honourable, and right, and pure, and lovely, and admirable. Think about things that are excellent and worthy of praise" (Philippians 4:8 NLT).

4.   Flee tempting situations.

It's a lot easier to live in purity if you avoid people, places, or situations that you know will make you vulnerable to temptation. Search your heart and steer clear of your personal areas of weakness.

5. Resist temptation boldly.

When temptation strikes, don't entertain it even briefly. Respond decisively by standing firm in God's truth about who you are in Christ and rejecting it, just like Jesus did (Matthew 4:1–11). Draw confidence from the Holy Spirit's power in you to overcome sin's influence.

6. Practise accountability.

Being surrounded by people who can lovingly support, encourage, and correct you is essential (Ecclesiastes 4:9–12). Have trusted friends who will pray with you and ask the hard questions as you pursue moral integrity. It's always better to fight alongside others than to struggle alone.

SCRIPTURES ABOUT PURITY

Psalm 51:10 (NLT)
"Create in me a clean heart, O God. Renew a loyal spirit within me."

2 Timothy 2:22 (NLT)
"Run from anything that stimulates youthful lusts. Instead, pursue righteous living, faithfulness, love, and peace. Enjoy the companionship of those who call on the Lord with pure hearts."

Matthew 5:8 (NLT)
"God blesses those whose hearts are pure, for they will see God."

1 Thessalonians 4:3–4 (NLT)
"God's will is for you to be holy, so stay away from all sexual sin. Then each of you will control his own body and live in holiness and honour."

Titus 2:11–12 (NLT)
"For the grace of God has been revealed, bringing salvation to all people. And we are instructed to turn from godless living and sinful pleasures. We should live in this evil world with wisdom, righteousness, and devotion to God."

GEORGE & JANET'S STORY

My name is George Akelo, and my wife's name is Janet. We are pastors of Home Church Kariobangi in Nairobi, Kenya, and I also serve as the Kenya Overseer for Home Church.

I was raised by great parents, but one time something happened. My dad married our stepmom, and this disoriented everything in the family, leading us into extreme poverty. Many days we had no food and no hope for the future. I faced many challenges— even living with friends when family situations became difficult. One of the places that I found refuge was in the slums of Nairobi. But it was in that same place of struggle that God found me and sent the right people who shaped my faith and belief. I found direction and purpose.

Through Home Church, I entered a training and discipleship programme where my faith grew and I was mentored for ministry. Out of that season, I helped start the Home of Hope Dream Centre, a baby rescue centre for abandoned children. What began as a place of hardship became the birthplace of God's vision to save lives.

During those early years in church, I met Janet. We met in a New Believers' class and found ourselves constantly serving together. Over time, our friendship deepened, and I knew she was the one. She is quiet, thoughtful, and full of wisdom. After seven years of friendship and courtship, we married in a beautiful church wedding.

Before marriage, we made a commitment to be pure. We chose not to kiss, hug, or allow physical closeness that could lead to temptation. It wasn't easy, but it built trust and deep respect between us. We kissed for the first time when we stood at the altar of marriage, and we had our honeymoon night in total blessing from both our parents and before God and the people.

We believe that setting strong boundaries helped us start our marriage with a clean heart and a clear conscience before God.

Today, we've been married for fourteen years, blessed with two biological children and six foster children from the Dream Centre—all rescued and supported by Canadian sponsors. Our lives are full of joy, purpose, and friendship. We continue to lead and serve together, helping others find the same freedom and hope we found in Christ.

Our message to young people is simple: Put God first, build friendship before romance, and live a life of purity. God has a great plan for your life.

THE BATTLE FOR YOUR GENERATION

Let's talk honestly about sex and purity. To understand what's gone wrong, we need to start with what sex was actually designed for.

God created sex as a gift, not a problem. Sex isn't bad—what's bad is how our culture has twisted it into something it was never meant to be.

Sex was designed as the ultimate connection between a husband and wife, uniting them spiritually, emotionally, and physically within marriage. That's the blueprint. Anything and everything outside those boundaries is sin, according to the Bible.

Unfortunately, the devil and our culture have presented sex as "cheap" and "casual." It's been deliberately reduced to just physical urges, stripped of its deeper meaning. This strategy, which comes straight from hell, has devastating consequences. When sex is disconnected from a loving marriage covenant, all kinds of negative things can happen:

- Unplanned pregnancies that can change one's life course
- STDs that can affect health for decades
- Rising sexual violence

- Skyrocketing divorce rates
- Emotional emptiness and inability to form deep connections
- Psychological trauma that can last a lifetime

To live in victory, we must understand where the battle really happens. God gave us a clear picture in Genesis 4:7: "Sin is crouching at your door" (NIV). Like a lion stalking its prey, sin waits for any opening, any moment of weakness. And when that weakness is found, the enemy will jump on it.

You have to be aware that sin is waiting to take you down. It's not a "little thing" that you can play with and then put down when you want. It becomes a life force that makes you its slave.

When I was a kid, we'd sing a song that said, "The devil is a sly old fox. If I could catch him, I'd put him in a box." As silly as that song was, its description is true. He is crafty and sly. He doesn't announce his intentions with warning signs. His strategy is much more subtle. He specializes in small compromises, those seemingly harmless choices that only cross small lines—at first.

James 1:14-15 tells us exactly how this works: "Temptation comes from our own desires, which entice us and drag us away. These desires give birth to sinful actions. And when sin is allowed to grow, it gives birth to death" (NLT). It's a progression that begins in your thoughts. The battlefield is in your mind, long before any physical action takes place.

Perhaps it's that internal negotiation about "technical virginity," convincing yourself you're still maintaining purity while pushing boundaries further and further. Or it's that choice to keep dating someone who gradually pulls you away from God, justifying it because they have "potential" to change.

These small compromises are like invisible threads in a spider's web. Each one seems insignificant on its own, but together they create a trap that's hard to escape. Each rationalization makes the next one easier. Each boundary pushed makes the following one less dramatic. Each justification weakens your resolve just a little more. Until one day you wake up far from where you ever thought you'd be, wondering how you got there.

This is why remembering that the devil is a sly old fox is so important. Because the journey away from purity rarely starts with big, obvious sins. It starts with small steps and quiet compromises.

NOTHING CASUAL ABOUT SEX

When God created sexual intimacy, He designed it as something awesome and incredible, a unique bond meant to unite a husband and wife not just physically, but emotionally and spiritually. At its core, it's meant to be other-centred, not self-centred. A gift that is at its absolute best in giving, not taking.

I've seen young people who gave their hearts away, piece by piece, now struggling to fully trust their spouses years later. The past betrayals created another reason to hold back emotionally. As Proverbs 4:23 warns us, "Above all else, guard your heart, for everything you do flows from it" (NIV). Those who didn't guard their hearts in their youth often spend years trying to rebuild what was carelessly given away.

Sex misused brings confusion where there should be clarity and emotional health. If you're tempted to compromise your moral stand, ask yourself these questions.

- Why give myself to the wrong person?
- Why wreck someone else's life?
- Why fall into Satan's trap of temptation?
- Why make a decision outside of God's timing for my life?
- Why waste my time in a relationship that is not God's will?

- Why put myself in a position of having to ask God for forgiveness for the sins I commit?
- Why set a wrong standard for my life that will affect my future and marriage?
- Why live with a guilty conscience when I can be pure?

Why not live according to the Bible? Faithfulness to God in your youth establishes the principle of faithfulness that will last a lifetime when you are married.

HELP! I'VE ALREADY FAILED

Maybe you're reading this and thinking, *It's too late for me.* You've made compromises. You've played with fire and got burned. While you can never get your virginity back, God can restore your purity and your calling.

David is a prime example from the Bible of someone who messed up. He fell into sexual sin with Bathsheba. His sin affected his life, from causing mistrust in the kingdom to separation in his family. That one decision led to very negative consequences, but God is a God of forgiveness. He will forgive you too!

When Nathan the prophet confronted David for his sin, he genuinely repented and asked God to restore to him the joy of his salvation. David's relationship with God was fully restored (Psalms 51). God then turned his failure into good, giving him a son with Bathsheba who became king of Israel. That son was Solomon, who was the wisest man to ever live and who wrote the 31 chapters of Proverbs that are our guide for daily living to this day.

WHAT STEPS CAN YOU TAKE?

First, get honest. The Bible says, "Confess your sins to one another" (James 5:16 NIV). This means stop minimizing sexual sin, acknowledge addiction, and face where you are at spiritually and morally.

Second, make a clean break. Scripture tells us, "don't let yourself think about ways to indulge your evil desires" (Romans 13:14 NLT). In today's world, this means end relationships that pull you from God, change phone numbers or social media accounts if necessary, and delete apps that lead to temptation.

Third, create new patterns. Begin each day in prayer before touching your phone. Build healthy habits and healthy friendships, and find positive activities that engage your mind.

Finally, get support. Connect with a mature Christian leader, practise accountability, seek Christian counselling if needed, be active in your church community, and remain faithful to God.

You will carry with you for the rest of your life the choices you make today regarding your body and what you do with it. The Bible says in 1 Corinthians 6:20 (NKJV), "For you were bought at a price; therefore glorify God in your body and in your spirit, which are God's."

The God who strengthened Joseph to flee temptation (Genesis 39:12), who restored David after failure (Psalm 51), and who transformed the Samaritan woman at the well (John 4) is ready to help you.

Make the choice today. Your future self will thank you.

CHANTELLE'S STORY:
UNYIELDING FOR THE KING

I never imagined that God would call me—a 25-year-old single female pastor—to participate in a reality dating TV show. Yet, God can use any means to reach the lost and broken and to bring salvation to the nation.

It all began with a simple purchase at Walmart. After finishing work one day, I stopped to pick up a few groceries when a lovely white summer dress caught my eye. I tried it on, and it fit perfectly. Although I didn't know when I would wear it, I bought it anyway. Later that evening, I drove to my parents' house for our weekly supper together. While watching TV after dinner, an advertisement flashed across the screen: "LIVE The Bachelor Canada Auditions coming to a city near you." The buzz in Canada was palpable as the popular show The Bachelor *was finally making its debut in the country. Thousands of single women across the nation had applied, and live auditions were happening in major cities.*

To my surprise, my dad—a devoted Christian who generally thinks little of reality shows—turned to me and said, "Chantelle, you should audition. They're coming to Calgary tomorrow! You love meeting new people and sharing Jesus with others. This is the perfect opportunity!" Calgary was only an hour away from my hometown.

I laughed and replied, "Sorry, Dad, but I work tomorrow, and no, I will not be trying out for a reality TV show."

Just then, my phone beeped. It was a text message from my boss, also a faithful follower of Jesus. He wrote, "Hi Chantelle, I just have this feeling you are supposed to take tomorrow off. Enjoy a nice day off from work."

I was flabbergasted! My boss had never given me a day off like that before. Suddenly, I remembered the white summer dress I had just purchased. With no excuses left, I sensed that the Lord was up to something.

"Okay, Dad, I'll go. But you're driving me!"

The next day, my dad dropped me off at the hotel in Calgary hosting the auditions. A sea of ladies were waiting in line. As I stood patiently, film crews and journalists moved through the crowd, meeting many of the ladies. When I approached the first table, they asked for my name, age, and occupation.

I replied, "My name is Chantelle Harink, I'm 25 years old, and I'm a pastor." You've never seen camera crews and journalists move so quickly! They rushed towards me, eager to know what it was like to be a pastor auditioning for a reality dating TV show. It was quite comical.

One of the cameramen and a journalist asked if they could film and document my entire audition journey. There were multiple waiting rooms, and if you made it through each round, you continued to the next. I met so many amazing women and had the opportunity to share my faith journey.

The day flew by, and I made it through the second round. When the film crew asked if I would advance to the final round, which required waiting several more hours, I gently declined. I needed to drive home in time to lead youth group at my church. They asked if I could come back tomorrow, but again, I had to turn them down due to work commitments.

As I started to leave, they eagerly requested just five more minutes of my time, and I agreed. They took me to a different part of the hotel, where only two girls were waiting outside a room. I was led inside, and a kind lady introduced herself as the casting director. To my shock, the gentleman beside her was the same man who had filmed me all day. I had thought he was a journalist cameraman, but he was the head of the film crew for The Bachelor!

The casting director interviewed me and then said goodbye. As I left, the cameraman gave me a big hug and whispered in my ear,

"We will see you soon."

In a daze, I found my dad waiting in the hotel lobby. When I approached him, he said, "You're going on the show, aren't you?"

I gathered my thoughts and, with a mix of fear and excitement, replied, "I think I am."

And he replied, "I knew you would."

There was a three-month wait until the auditions closed. I wrestled with the idea of whether I would accept an offer to be on the show. I spoke to my mentors, who were in their 70s and had been pastors their entire lives. After praying together, they quoted Esther 4:14b: "Who can say but that God has brought you into the palace for just such a time as this?" They reminded me of Esther's story, where she had to go before the king to save a nation.

God was telling me it was my time to step forward and be bold in my faith and purity. As a virgin with minimal dating experience, going on a dating reality show was far outside my comfort zone. But God often uses people in mysterious ways, and this was just one of the ways He intended to use me.

I fasted and prayed, inviting others to join me. I wanted to ensure that God's favour and presence were with me. I kept hearing, "For such a time as this."

Finally, the day came when I received the call from The Bachelor Canada*: I had been chosen as one of the bachelorettes for the very first season! I had 24 hours to decide, but I couldn't tell anyone. I spent the night praying, asking God to make it clear if I was meant to participate. If I went on the show, I would be leaving work for three months. I needed to ask my boss for the time off. However, when my boss found out I had auditioned for a reality TV show, he was not pleased. I knew it would be a miracle for him to say yes to letting me go. I asked God that if I was to go, to have my boss say these exact words: You have my blessing.*

The next day, I entered my boss's office early and shared my heart and why I felt called to the show. With tears in his eyes, he took my hands and said, "You have my blessing." I broke down crying, knowing this was truly God's leading. As scared as I was, I felt assured that God would be with me on the show—and He was.

My experience on the show was both challenging and beautiful. I made incredible friends in the Bachelor Mansion. One day, out of boredom, the film crew asked me to preach a message. The Holy Spirit moved as I shared, resulting in a miraculous healing—a girl's back was healed, and hard hearts softened towards Jesus. The entire film crew was in tears being moved by the presence of God. There were so many amazing God moments behind the scenes that never made it onto TV.

A pivotal moment on the show came when I was encouraged to share on national television that I was a virgin. Although hesitant, on a date with the bachelor, I shared that I was a virgin and I was saving sex for marriage. God used that moment to impact the girls in the mansion as well as many viewers. After the show, I received invitations to speak at churches, community events, radio stations, and marriage conventions about the importance of staying pure before marriage.

After two months living in the Bachelor Mansion, I received a call from my dad informing me that my grandpa had suddenly passed away. I had to make a choice: stay on the show or go home. I knew it was time to leave. The bachelor was a great guy but not currently serving the Lord. I was confident that God had someone incredible for me—and He did.

Shortly after the show, I reconnected with a schoolmate, Jory Young. He had never dated and had also chosen to remain pure until marriage. Now, ten years later, we have four beautiful children and have the joy of pastoring together in the kids' ministry programme at Home Church Red Deer.

—Chantelle

QUESTIONS FOR REFLECTION

1. Have you established moral standards for your life?

2. Are there two or three trusted people who could help keep you accountable in this area? Write their names here. When will you ask them for help?

3. What boundaries do you need to set for relationships, social media, and entertainment to protect your purity?

4. What past choices or patterns do you need to bring into the light so that healing and freedom can begin? What step will you take this week to start that process?

5. What practices or habits can you build into your daily routine that will strengthen your commitment to purity and keep your heart aligned with God's design?

NOTES

PURITY

CHOICE 6

TRUTH

The truth is knowing Jesus.

MY STORY

I called my favourite taxi driver to take me from our condo in Calgary to the airport for another international ministry trip. Sitting in the back seat of the cab, I engaged the driver in conversation about his faith in God. Because he was from the Philippines, I assumed he was a Roman Catholic and had some faith in Jesus. I shared with him my faith in God and how I had come to personal salvation through accepting Jesus as my Lord and Saviour.

He said, "I am a Muslim, and Jesus is our prophet."

I then asked him about his wife and her faith. "Is she a Muslim too?" I asked.

He said, "No, she is a born-again Christian and she told me she is a member of a great Filipino church in Calgary."

I then shared with him that the Jesus he had was a different Jesus than his wife had. She believed that Jesus is the eternal Son of God, and I invited him to experience for himself the born-again experience.

What struck me most was his sincere belief that we were both serving the same God, just in different ways. In that moment, I realised something profound—he wanted truth to be whatever he defined it to be. But truth isn't something we create or define. It's established by God Himself.

You see, this conversation wasn't just about different religious views. It revealed a crucial principle about truth that's especially relevant today: Truth isn't subjective or personal. It's not like choosing what flavour of ice cream you prefer. Truth is absolute because it comes from an absolute God.

Jesus tells us frankly in John 14:6: "I am the way, the truth, and the life. No one comes to the Father except through me" (NKJV). Jesus didn't present Himself as one option among many. He claimed to be the exclusive path to knowing God.

A good question that I might ask you is: **Do you know Jesus who is "the way, the truth, and the life"?**

WHAT IS TRUTH?

This reminds me of three young men in the Bible who understood the cost of standing for truth. Shadrach, Meshach, and Abednego were teenagers when they were taken from their Jewish homeland to Babylon. Despite being trained for the king's service, they refused to compromise their convictions when Nebuchadnezzar demanded they bow to his golden idol.

Think about this: These young men chose possible death over denying what they knew to be true. They had no guarantee that God would rescue them, yet they stood firm. Their example challenges us today. In a culture that wants us to reshape truth to fit popular opinion, we must choose whether we'll stand for God's unchanging truth or bow to the pressure of our age.

This brings us to one of the most crucial questions we face today: What is truth? Over the years, I've watched our culture shift dramatically from believing in absolute truth to embracing what I call "designer truth" or what sociology calls radical relativism—where everyone creates their own version of what's true. Every person has a licence to construct their own personal "truth" and then fiercely defend it as "sacred."

And if that weren't bad enough, we've now reached a point where challenging someone's personal "truth" is often labelled as "hate" or "intolerance." But let me ask you something: If your truth contradicts my truth, and both of us claim to be right, how can that possibly work? It's like having multiple drivers at an intersection, each believing they have the right of way. Chaos and collision are inevitable.

There is an urgent need for a truth that stands apart from our own limited opinions, emotions, and preferences. A truth that serves as an objective standard against which all claims and beliefs can be measured. Without such an absolute truth, we are left adrift in a sea of subjectivity. Truth becomes changeable and relative, open to individual interpretation and the ebb and flow of cultural tides.

The Bible makes a bold claim in John 17:17 (NKJV): "Your word is truth." Not *a* truth, not *some* truth, but truth itself. When Jesus said, "I am the truth," He was declaring Himself as the standard by which everything else is measured.

Truth isn't just an external set of rules. Rather, God has placed within each of us what John 1:9 calls "the true light that gives light to everyone" (NIV), or an internal compass pointing towards truth. That's why even in cultures that have never heard of the Bible, people still have a natural sense of right and wrong.

KARNEL'S STORY
Kazakhstan

My journey to Christ began in my childhood. When I was four years old, I started going to church with my aunt. Back then, church was nothing more than a place to socialize with children from Christian families and receive gifts on holidays. I stopped going to church when I became a teenager—it no longer felt like a fun place, so I stopped going.

Throughout my childhood, I was caught between two worlds. My father is a Turkish Muslim, while my mother and aunt are Russian Christians.

My dad never forbade me from going to church, but he wasn't exactly thrilled about it either. He always gave me the freedom to choose—whether to become a Christian or a Muslim was entirely up to me. And eventually, that moment of choice came into my life.

After finishing school, I moved to pursue higher education, and I met a girl whom I fell deeply in love with. But because of our strong and difficult personalities, I stopped seeing a future with her. That's when the Lord opened my eyes and mind. A fire was lit inside me that I couldn't explain:

"I must get to know the Lord!"

I suggested to my girlfriend that we seek the Lord together, because she also sensed that something wasn't right in our relationship. We decided to start looking for God through Christianity, since we were both familiar with the religion—but we didn't know Christ.

I began to pray and call out to the Lord in the way I had been taught as a child. I prayed and asked Him to free me from fear, to free me from anxiety. I asked the Lord to change me and my behaviour towards my loved ones.

I started to search historical evidence and compare the Bible with the Quran. I had to find out who Jesus is. I studied it for about a year, and I came to the point where I could no longer reject that Jesus is the Saviour.

I called out to Jesus and said to him in prayer, "If you are my Saviour and God, take my anxiety and stress and change me." In a short period of time, I felt that my prayers were answered and Jesus came into my life.

The Saviour came with the message of love. This was the beginning of my transformation and my true encounter with Christ.

Through personal study and prayer, Christ began to free me from fear and anxiety. The Lord healed our relationship and brought peace into my heart. I began to strengthen my faith by studying the history and prophecies about the coming of the Saviour.

And that's how I made my final decision—that I want to dedicate my life to Him. Then shortly after I got baptized. And I keep growing in my faith with serving Jesus.

—Karnel

SCRIPTURES ABOUT TRUTH

Psalm 86:11 (NLT)
"Teach me your ways, O Lord, that I may live according to your truth! Grant me purity of heart, so that I may honour you."

Ephesians 4:15 (NLT)
"Instead, we will speak the truth in love, growing in every way more and more like Christ, who is the head of his body, the church."

Zechariah 8:16 (NLT)
"But this is what you must do: Tell the truth to each other. Render verdicts in your courts that are just and that lead to peace."

3 John 1:4 (NLT)
"I could have no greater joy than to hear that my children are following the truth."

COMMIT TO TRUTH

All the confusion that faces us today started with a simple question: "Did God really say...?" (Genesis 3:1 NIV). That's how Satan planted the first seed of doubt in Eve's mind, and humanity has been wrestling with deception ever since.

I've watched this pattern repeat itself countless times. From that first lie in the Garden, deception has spread like a virus, infecting every area of human life. It reshapes societies, distorts reality, and alters the course of history. The deeper we go into deception, the harder it becomes to recognise truth.

The digital age has supercharged this problem. Take the COVID-19 pandemic—we witnessed how quickly lies and conspiracy theories could spread across the globe. Social media became a breeding ground for misinformation, with hidden agendas disguised as facts.

The climate change debate offers another sobering example. Rather than engaging with verifiable scientific evidence, many influential voices choose to manipulate public opinion through deception. Politics often triumphs over truth, leaving society more confused and divided than ever.

Here's what's at stake: When we accept lies as truth and dismiss truth as lies, we erode the very foundation society stands on. Trust breaks down. Communities fragment. Our pursuit of knowledge and progress gets derailed.

The consequences of falling for deception go far beyond just being wrong about something. Every lie we believe limits our ability to experience the freedom and good life God intended for us.

As followers of Christ, we must anchor ourselves firmly in biblical truth. I've seen how only God's revealed truth in Scripture can help us accurately distinguish between light and darkness, between what's eternal and what's temporary, and between what is right and what is wrong.

The Bible stands as our supreme authority for faith and life. It provides an unwavering standard against which we can measure every claim, ideology, and teaching that comes our way. Unlike public opinion or cultural trends that shift like sand, Scripture remains rock-solid.

Consider something as fundamental as marriage. Throughout history and culture, marriage has been redefined countless times. But God's Word illustrates that marriage isn't just a human tradition we can remake as we please. From the very beginning, God established it as a sacred covenant between one man and one woman, giving them the mandate to "be fruitful and multiply" (Genesis 1:28).

I'm deeply concerned for every young person today. You're facing a tsunami of competing worldviews, each claiming to be true. Social media bombards you with messages that contradict God's Word. That's why it's essential to root your convictions in Scripture. Without this foundation, you'll find yourself swept along by whatever sounds good in the moment.

God has given humanity the precious gift of free will, which is the ability to choose what we believe. But these choices carry eternal consequences. One day, each of us will stand before God and give account for the beliefs we embraced and the choices we made. These decisions will result in either eternal life with Him or eternal separation from His presence.

HOW DO WE LIVE IN TRUTH?

Knowing truth and living truth are two very different things. It's not enough to simply agree that truth exists—we must align our entire lives with it. That's where real transformation begins.

I often wonder what Jesus would say if He were pastoring a church today. I believe He'd welcome everyone with open arms, extending friendship and love to all who came through the doors. But He wouldn't stop there. Just as He did in the Gospels, He'd call each person to a life of obedience. Truth isn't just something we believe. It's a path we walk.

"You will know the truth, and the truth will set you free" (John 8:32 NIV). These words of Jesus reveal something profound about truth's power. But this freedom isn't about doing whatever we want. True freedom comes from living in alignment with God's design. Every time we choose lies over truth, we actually wrap ourselves in chains of bondage.

The world around us is growing darker with deception. Isaiah prophesied this would happen—that darkness would cover the earth, but God's light would still shine (Isaiah 60:2). We shouldn't live in fear, but we should commit to seeking God's truth. This requires spiritual discernment. We can't accept everything at face value. Every message, every teaching, every cultural trend must be measured against the standard of God's Word. This calls for genuine repentance—for turning away from the lies we've believed and embracing God's truth wholeheartedly.

The Bible provides clear "yes" and "no" guidance for life. While our feelings fluctuate and desires shift, God's Word remains steady. It's our reliable compass, steering us away from deception's quicksand onto truth's solid ground.

When we choose to live by truth rather than feelings, we discover the very freedom our hearts have always longed for. That's the power of truth. That's the life God designed us to live.

I've never seen anyone regret building their life on God's truth, but I've counselled countless people devastated by believing lies. Truth isn't always comfortable—it often challenges our preferences and confronts our desires. But it always leads to freedom.

In our world today, standing for truth comes at a cost. Like those three young men facing Nebuchadnezzar's furnace, we must decide what we value more—cultural acceptance or divine truth.

The pressure to compromise grows stronger by the day. The voices calling truth "hate" and lies "love" grow louder. But truth remains truth, regardless of popular opinion.

Every great move of God throughout history began when people returned to His truth. Not partial truth. Not modified truth. Not culturally acceptable truth. But the pure, unchanging truth of God's Word. That's what transformed lives in the first century, and that's what transforms lives today.

To every young person wrestling with these issues: Don't let anyone tell you that truth is outdated or irrelevant. What you believe shapes who you become. The choices you make about truth today will echo through your tomorrow. Choose wisely. Stand firmly. Walk confidently in God's truth.

Remember, Jesus didn't say "I am a truth" or even "I have truth." He declared "I am THE truth." In a world drowning in relative truth and personal opinion, He stands as our absolute reference point. When we align our lives with Him, everything else falls into proper perspective.

In the end, truth doesn't just set us free—it keeps us free. That's worth everything it costs us to stand for it.

DAVID'S STORY

I'm 19 years old, and I'm from Uzbekistan. I was born in a pastor's family. Since childhood, our family has faced persecution, and that's the environment I grew up in.

Until I was seven, no one told me about God. But later, my parents decided to tell me about Jesus Christ and started hosting a children's ministry at our home. At the time, I didn't understand much, but later I began attending youth services.

When I turned 13, we had a youth event called "Encounter with God." During that event, we wrote our sins and bad habits on pieces of paper and nailed them to a cross, symbolizing that it was our sins that crucified Jesus. In that moment, I asked God for forgiveness, dedicated my life to Him, and decided to serve Him for the rest of my life.

Since I was born in a Muslim country, all of my childhood friends were Muslim. They would tell me about Islam, and I would share with them what I knew about Christianity. That was when a real spiritual battle for my soul began. I started asking serious questions: "What is truth?" "Could Jesus really be God?" "Who even asked Jesus to die for someone?"

My friends were devout Muslims —they didn't smoke, drink, or curse. Their families had clear rules, and they followed them strictly. Their way of life inspired me, especially since I was quite the troublemaker back then and loved drawing attention to myself.

But everything changed when I had a personal encounter with God. I began to pray in secret, seeking His face. And God began revealing truth to me. One particular verse kept capturing my attention: "Jesus said to him, 'I am the way, the truth, and the life. No one comes to the Father except through Me'" (John 14:6).

In this verse, Jesus clearly says that only through Him can we come to the Father. There is no other way—not through another religion, not through good deeds, not through traditions. Only Him.

I began to study the life of Jesus more deeply and understand why He chose to die for us. In Isaiah chapter 53, I found something incredible—the depth of God's love. It clearly says that God was willing to give His One and Only Son for us. He took on our sicknesses, bore our suffering, and died in our place.

No other religion reveals such love or such a sacrifice.

That's when I made a decision: I choose life with Jesus. I want to live the rest of my life with Him!

—David

QUESTIONS FOR REFLECTION

1. What lies have you been believing about yourself, God, or your future that contradict the Bible? What is the truth?

2. When was the last time you stood up for biblical truth, even when it was unpopular? If you've been silent, what held you back?

3. Name three examples of how our culture's mindset tries to influence your decisions about relationships, sexuality, or identity.

4. Which parts of the Bible do you find most difficult to accept as absolute truth? Will you commit to studying these passages more deeply rather than dismissing them?

5. How much time do you spend daily filling your mind with Scripture compared to social media, entertainment, or other voices? Based on this chapter, what specific change will you make to this ratio, starting today?

NOTES

CHOICE 7

MORE THAN ENOUGH

A prosperous life

MY STORY

I walked to the back of the conference and said to a minister, "Welcome to the conference." My pastor friend, Steve, had informed me that the friend he brought to the conference had a different set of beliefs and values from mine, but I was still shocked at the abrupt answer to my welcome.

He said, "So you are one of those prosperity preachers, are you?"

I smiled and replied, "Sir, let me explain by asking you a question. When someone gets saved and experiences the abundant life that Jesus offers, will life become better for him?"

He answered, "Well, of course."

"When a person gets saved and starts experiencing the renewing of the mind, will he have better thoughts and emotions and make better decisions?

"Yes."

"And when a person has better thoughts and emotions, and when he begins to make better decisions, is it possible that with making better decisions, he will have more money and a more prosperous life?"

He said, "Yes."

"That's what I believe about prosperity."

When Heather and I moved to Red Deer in 1972 we had very little. I had one suit, she had one nice dress, and we ate off chipped, stained, and borrowed dishes in a basement suite where the toilet often didn't flush and the cupboards were held together with string. For several years in the early days of our church, we lived in scarcity, but God was faithful, and somehow we got through life just scraping through from month to month.

I'll never forget one particular day, sitting down for another low-quality supper meal of mac-and-cheese—again. We had soup or mac-and-cheese with some tuna fish added to make it extra special because it was inexpensive and all we could afford. But that day, something in me snapped. I had changed my mindset.

I slammed down my spoon on the table and declared to my wife and kids, "I'm done struggling to have just enough. I'm done with a life of poverty and just having enough. God has bigger and better plans for us."

Several months before this experience I had been reading the Bible and discovered that God was a God of great provision. I discovered that there are three levels of living.

Level 1: The Land of Poverty. The children of Israel lived in poverty for 400 years, enslaved in Egypt.

Level 2: The Land of Just Enough. God delivered them from Egypt and they journeyed into the wilderness, where they always had just enough to survive.

Level 3: The Land of More Than Enough. God promised the children of Israel that they would live in a land of milk and honey, with wells they had not dug and houses they had not built. God's plan was a land of abundance and plenty.

I discovered from the Scripture that Jesus became poor that we might become rich, spiritually, emotionally, relationally, and financially: "For you know the grace of our Lord Jesus Christ, that though he was rich, yet for your sake he became poor, so that you through his poverty might become rich" (2 Corinthians 8:9 NIV). God's plan is not poverty, because Jesus died on the cross and dealt with poverty as part of our salvation. Now He wants to supply our need according to His riches in glory (Philippians 4:19) and lead us to the land of plenty.

So I made a vow to change my thinking. I was determined to pursue a more biblical mindset about God, myself, and the world around me. I knew I couldn't keep living paycheck-to-paycheck, always anxious about whether we'd have enough.

In Scripture, Abraham's journey from scarcity to flourishing provides a powerful example for us today. When God first called him and made incredible promises about becoming a great nation and blessing all peoples on earth (Genesis 12:2-3), Abraham may have struggled to fully embrace this successful mindset.

Initially, his thoughts were limited by what he could see—his childlessness, the famine in Canaan, his advanced age. But God consistently challenged Abraham to think bigger, to align his mindset with divine promises rather than earthly circumstances.

The turning point came when "Abraham believed the Lord, and He credited it to him as righteousness" (Genesis 15:6 NIV). This wasn't just about believing God existed—it was about believing God's promise of prosperity and abundance. Abraham had to intentionally move from thinking in terms of lack to thinking in terms of God's unlimited provision. His mind shifted when God took him out of his tent and told him to look at the stars in the sky. God told him that in 400 years, his children would inherit and possess the Promised Land. In other words, he was saying, "Abraham, think bigger."

This transformed mindset can be seen years later when God tested Abraham with Isaac. When Abraham said, "God himself will provide" (Genesis 22:8 NIV), it shows he had fully embraced God's promises. His willingness to line up his thinking with God's promises opened the door for blessing that would impact all nations.

It's important that you challenge and change your thinking because if you believe that God is a taskmaster who wants you to struggle through life, then it will be impossible for you to step out in faith and do the purpose God put you on the planet for. You must believe that you serve a big God who has big plans for you and big blessings in store for you. And his blessings are not just for you— they are for you to be a blessing to everyone around you.

HOW SUCCESSFUL LIVING BEGINS

Spiritually, successful living really begins with giving your heart to God, making Jesus the Lord of your life, and then living according to the Word of God. That's the first step.

Financially, it begins with giving God your first and your best, which the Bible describes as the tithe. Tithing means giving God 10 percent of your income.

My mother taught me to tithe when I was just a child. She took a dime and broke it down into ten pennies, then said, "Son, this first penny is the Lord's. The rest you can use for yourself."

When I delivered papers as a young boy, I practiced tithing. When I took my first job at age 13, working in the meat department of the Estevan Co-op, the first action I took after receiving my first paycheck was to give God 10 percent.

I'm happy to say that God has been faithful and we have always lived with His provision. Since then, as I have continued to believe what He says in His Word, I have had the privilege of seeing His church experience miracle after miracle in the many nations where I work.

CHANGE YOUR MINDSET, CHANGE YOUR LIFE

Our thoughts shape our lives in deep, long-lasting ways. The perspectives and mindsets we hold influence every decision we make and every path we take. I learned this truth through my own journey.

Growing up in poverty, I developed what I called a survival mentality—a mindset focused on just getting by with barely enough. Instead of abundance, my young mind knew only scarcity. Just enough food. Just enough clothing. Just enough to pay the bills. This sense of lack and constant struggle became deeply rooted in my thinking.

When God called me to ministry as a young man, my poverty mindset followed me. Looking around at the pastors I knew, all living in poor conditions, I resigned myself to what seemed inevitable: While on earth, I would live in poverty, but one day I would walk on streets of gold. I had settled this in my mind as my unchangeable future.

But when I began to read the Bible with fresh eyes, I discovered a different picture: from Genesis 2, where the garden overflowed with abundance, to Abraham's story of prosperity even in the midst of trials. I saw God's promises to Israel: "The Lord will make you the head, not the tail. If you pay attention to the commands of the Lord your God... you will always be at the top, never at the bottom" (Deuteronomy 28:13 NIV).

Throughout Scripture, I encountered a God of abundance, not scarcity. Even Jesus's sacrifice pointed to this truth. He became poor so that we might become rich, not just spiritually, but emotionally, relationally, and in all areas of life.

Over time, my mind began to renew. The transformation wasn't instant, but as I aligned my thoughts with God's truth, everything began to change. I'm so grateful I didn't stay stuck in that mental place of scarcity!

This is exactly what Paul meant when he wrote, "Let God transform you into a new person by changing the way you think" (Romans 12:2 NIV). Real, lasting change begins with a renewal of the mind. This isn't about positive thinking or wishful dreams, but about allowing God to reshape our thought patterns according to His infinite wisdom and perfect perspective.

I admit, this process of renewing my mind was not easy. I had to work at it diligently. I read uplifting books and surrounded myself with positive people. I wrote out encouraging Scriptures and affirmations on cards, reading them daily and striving to live by those truths throughout the day.

I had to shake off complacency, wrestle against wrong thinking, and stretch myself into new places of faith. When I finally broke free from that cocoon of negative thought patterns, I began to fly. I experienced a radical transformation of the mind. And when I changed my mind, I changed my life. As I often say, "It's time to change your stinking thinking!"

SCRIPTURES ABOUT PROSPERITY

Proverbs 10:22 (NLT)
"The blessing of the Lord makes a person rich,
and he adds no sorrow with it."

Proverbs 11:25 (NLT)
"The generous will prosper;
those who refresh others will themselves be refreshed."

Deuteronomy 8:18 (NLT)
"Remember the Lord your God. He is the one who gives you power to be successful, in order to fulfil the covenant he confirmed to your ancestors with an oath."

Philippians 4:19 (NLT)

"And this same God who takes care of me will supply all your needs from his glorious riches, which have been given to us in Christ Jesus."

Psalm 112:1–3 NIV

"Praise the Lord!
How joyful are those who fear the Lord
and delight in obeying his commands.
Their children will be successful everywhere;
an entire generation of godly people will be blessed.
They themselves will be wealthy,
and their good deeds will last forever."

3 John 1:2 (NKJV)

"Beloved, I pray that you may prosper in all things and be in health, just as your soul prospers."

TEN LIFE-CHANGING THOUGHTS

What thoughts and perspectives do we need to adopt to experience this kind of mind renewal? Here are ten powerful truths that can reframe your mindset for prosperity.

1. God has big plans for me.

God doesn't create small plans for His children. When He called Abraham, He spoke about nations and generations—not just individual blessing. That same God has purposes for your life that are greater than what you can currently see.

I remember the day God challenged my limited thinking through a respected minister who said, "Stop measuring your future possibilities against your present limitations." That statement opened my eyes. Like Joseph in prison, I had allowed my circumstances to shape my expectations instead of trusting God's promises.

God has a long history of taking people from simple beginnings to remarkable destinies. He lifted Joseph from the pit to the palace, David from the shepherd's field to the throne, and Moses from the desert to leading a nation. These stories remind us that God works powerfully through those who trust His greater plan.

2. I am blessed to be a blessing.

God's prosperity always carries divine purpose. When He blessed Abraham, He said, "I will bless you... and you will be a blessing" (Genesis 12:2 NIV). This shows us a key kingdom principle: God's blessing is meant to flow through us, not merely to us.

As God began enlarging our ministry, He taught us this essential truth: *His provision was never intended for personal accumulation, but for kingdom multiplication.* Just as He gave Israel wells they didn't dig and vineyards they didn't plant, God provides abundance so we can extend His goodness to others.

With prosperity comes responsibility. Instead of holding tightly to what God gives, we become channels of His generosity. In God's kingdom, increase is always connected to purpose.

3. God empowers me to take risks.

"The wicked man flees though no one pursues, but the righteous are as bold as a lion" (Proverbs 28:1 NIV). God's prosperity mindset is about stepping out in faith when He calls.

I've learned that comfort zones rarely lead to the Promised Land. Every significant blessing in my life came after a moment when I had to decide: Will I trust God's leading or my own fear? Just as Peter had to step out of the boat to walk on water, prosperity often waits on the other side of your greatest risk.

The Bible is filled with risk-takers who followed God's voice: Noah building an ark before rain existed, Joshua marching around Jericho, Esther approaching the king uninvited. Their obedience opened doors to God's supernatural provision. Remember that faith is the currency of heaven, and sometimes your greatest investment is the courage to obey when God says "Go."

4.   I am called to start, not just serve.

"Whatever you do, work at it with all your heart, as working for the Lord, not for human masters" (Colossians 3:23 NIV). God hasn't just called you to clock in and clock out—He's given you gifts to create, build, and establish.

When God created mankind, His first instruction was to be fruitful and multiply and to have dominion. This creative, entrepreneurial spirit reflects God's own nature. He is creative, productive, and abundant.

Whether it involves starting a business, launching a ministry, or developing the talents God has given you, prosperity often grows out of creating value for others. Don't settle for only benefiting from what others have built. Become someone who produces, contributes, and brings new blessing into the world.

5.   I must set clear, faith-filled goals.

"Write the vision and make it plain on tablets, that he may run who reads it" (Habakkuk 2:2 NKJV). Prosperity follows those who know where they're going and why.

Vague hopes produce vague results. I've learned that God honours specific prayers and defined targets. Jesus didn't just tell the blind man, "May you feel better." He asked, "What do you want me to do for you?" (Mark 10:51 NIV). Clear vision creates momentum.

Setting God-inspired goals isn't arrogance—it's wisdom. When David prepared to build the temple, he gathered specific materials. When Nehemiah rebuilt Jerusalem's walls, he created detailed plans. Your prosperity journey needs the same kind of clarity. What career path will you take? What income can you create? How can you stay out of debt and build your savings? Make it specific and measurable, and watch God direct your steps.

6.   I need God's vision, not just my own.

"Where there is no vision, the people perish" (Proverbs 29:18 KJV). True prosperity begins with seeing life through God's perspective, not our limited view.

Vision is about aligning your future with what God has already purposed. When Moses stood before the burning bush, God didn't ask for Moses' five-year plan—He revealed His divine intention to deliver Israel. Prosperity flows when we catch God's vision for our lives.

I've learned that time spent in prayer and in God's Word sharpens my vision. Just as binoculars need to be adjusted to see clearly, our spiritual sight must be brought into focus with heaven's perspective. Don't settle for success that lacks divine purpose. Ask God to show you what He sees for your career, your family, your ministry, and your future.

7. I honour God with my firstfruits through tithing.

"Honour the LORD with your wealth, with the firstfruits of all your crops; then your barns will be filled to overflowing, and your vats will brim over with new wine" (Proverbs 3:9-10 NIV). Tithing isn't just a religious ritual—it's a prosperity principle that positions your finances for blessing.

When we give God the first tenth of our increase, we recognise His authority over all we have. It's a practical demonstration that we trust Him more than our money. Malachi 3:10 is the only place in Scripture where God commands us to test him. He invites us to prove His faithfulness through our giving.

I've watched this principle work over and over in my own life. During seasons when our finances were especially tight, tithing didn't always make sense, yet it consistently opened the door for God's supernatural provision. God doesn't ask for your money because He needs it—He asks because He wants your heart. Tithing reveals who truly holds first place in your financial priorities.

8. I sow generously when I see a need.

"Remember this: Whoever sows sparingly will also reap sparingly, and whoever sows generously will also reap generously" (2 Corinthians 9:6 NIV). Prosperity grows when we respond to needs with generosity instead of fear.

God's kingdom doesn't operate the same way the world does. In His economy, giving isn't losing—it's planting. Every generous action becomes a seed that brings a future harvest. I've seen this happen many times: when we chose to help others even during our own difficult seasons, God provided in ways we never expected.

Jesus showed us this principle when He fed thousands with a boy's small lunch. Instead of holding onto what little He had, He blessed it, broke it, and shared it. Then it multiplied. That's how God works. What we willingly place in His hands becomes something far greater. Many of your biggest breakthroughs will come right after your most sacrificial moments of giving.

9. I value financial wisdom and discipline.

"The plans of the diligent lead to profit as surely as haste leads to poverty" (Proverbs 21:5 NIV). Real, God-honouring success happens when spiritual principles meet practical wisdom. Some people think that making a financial plan means you don't have faith. But the Bible talks a lot about wise planning—budgeting, saving, and managing what God gives us. Joseph created a fourteen-year plan that saved nations. The Proverbs 31 woman made smart investments and handled her resources wisely.

I've learned that prosperity takes both God's supernatural help and our own everyday responsibility. We pray for daily bread, but we also work hard. We trust God to provide, but we also make realistic budgets. We believe God for the right opportunities, but we also build real skills.

True prosperity shows up when God's power meets our willingness to be disciplined and responsible.

10. I understand that prosperity extends beyond finances.

"Beloved, I pray that you may prosper in all things and be in health, just as your soul prospers" (3 John 1:2 NKJV). God's abundance affects every part of life, not just your bank account.

True biblical prosperity includes strong health, meaningful relationships, peace of mind, and spiritual strength. A person with millions but no peace, broken relationships, or compromised health isn't truly prosperous. God's blessing is holistic, which means it touches every area of life.

This balanced view protects us from both materialism and unhealthy attitudes towards wealth. We neither worship money nor fear it. Instead, we seek God's kingdom first, trusting that everything we need—provision, health, relationships, and purpose—will be added as we follow Him wholeheartedly. True prosperity means having enough to fulfil your God-given purpose and enough to share with others along the way.

LIVING A LIFE WITHOUT LIMITS

Looking back at that defining moment over our mac-and-cheese dinner, I could never have imagined the journey God would take us on. What began with a simple decision to change my thinking has blossomed into a life of abundance that continues to amaze me daily. Heather and I have travelled the world and been able to bless many people as we learned to walk in God's blessings.

God's prosperity is a lifestyle of living aligned with His kingdom principles. The transformation doesn't happen overnight. For me, it began with replacing one limiting thought with one truth from Scripture. Then another. Then another. These small shifts in thinking eventually created dramatic changes in my circumstances.

The beauty of God's prosperity plan is that it works no matter who you are or where you're starting from. Whether you're struggling to pay bills or managing millions, these principles apply universally because they're based on eternal truths, not temporary trends. Joseph applied them in Potiphar's prison and Pharaoh's palace. David implemented them as both a shepherd boy and a king. Ruth practiced them as a widowed immigrant and as the wife of a wealthy landowner.

As I close this chapter, I want to challenge you to evaluate your own thinking about success. What limitations have you accepted as unchangeable facts? Where have experiences from your past caused you to stop believing for abundance?

My prayer for you comes from 3 John 1:2, that you would "prosper in all things and be in health, just as your soul prospers" (NKJV). May you embrace God's abundant vision for your life, walking in the blessing that enables you not only to meet your own needs but to become a channel of His generosity to a world in desperate need of hope.

ANUAR'S STORY

I grew up in a Christian household, where the church was always central to our family. My parents were a great example of faith, which shaped me early on, and although I can't point to one exact moment when I firmly gave my life to Jesus, what I do know is that their consistency kept me close to the church, and eventually it became personal for me.

In 2013, my family immigrated to Canada, and it completely flipped our lives upside down. We left everything we knew and had to start over from scratch. It was not easy, but when we came, we made a deliberate choice to settle in Red Deer because of Home Church. We wanted to plant our family in a good church and community. Looking back now, we still say it was one of the best decisions our family has ever made. Nothing was more important to us than Jesus and His church, and we've seen firsthand that when you pursue God's house, blessing follows. He opens doors, He brings the right people, and He creates opportunities you never could have made happen on your own.

When I entered my early twenties and got married, Nicole and I knew we had to build our careers in a way that positioned us to bless the church financially. One of our goals as a couple was to become kingdom builders, to serve and impact people around us, whether by giving towards projects in the church or by encouraging the people in our lives. It was a new purpose for us, and I was determined to make some changes. I was still deeply involved in church, but I realised I wanted to give more than just my time, especially since I had less of it. There are usually enough people with free time, but there are fewer who position themselves to bless the church financially. I wanted to be one of those people. We must choose to act. Faith without works is dead, so I set goals and got practical. I spent time with people I admired, especially Ryan Gaunce and Troy Walker, listening closely, asking for advice, and acting on it. I did not want to look back and regret not taking on opportunities and risks.

Right after we got married, one of the most significant practical decisions we made was to downsize. We sold unnecessary items, such as an extra vehicle, and cut back wherever possible. We did not mind being uncomfortable as long as it meant our lives would keep moving forward. One of the most significant steps we took was moving out of our newly renovated home into a 552-square-foot apartment so we could save and invest. We ran Airbnb from the main suite, rented out the basement, and put everything extra aside. During this season, we both worked full-time while I was in school to get my business degree.

After some time in the apartment, we purchased another property to move to and finally settled in. Not long after, an unexpected pipe burst flooded the basement suite. We lost our tenants, and the insurance did not fully cover the costly repair, making it feel like a significant setback. But we did not stop there. Around the same time, we received an Airbnb booking for a very extended stay at the highest monthly rate we had ever charged, but our Airbnb property was already booked. I saw the opportunity and rented them the upstairs suite of the new property instead. To make it work, Nicole and I moved in with my parents for what we thought would be only a few weeks, hoping to move into the basement suite once it was finished.

Unfortunately, the renovation company we hired ran into issues, and one of their contractors stole all of our materials and disappeared. What was supposed to be a two-week job stretched into four months. Living with my parents meant a tiny room that only fit a single bed. Nicole slept on the bed, and I slept on the floor. When the renovation was finally done, we moved into the basement suite ourselves with a plan to take back the upstairs once the guests moved out. But when the time came, we realised it made more financial sense to keep renting the upstairs and stay in the basement.

At the same time, I was working under Ryan and learning the industry. I quickly realised that if I was going to succeed, I had to become the best I could be at what I do. That meant spending long hours with Ryan, paying attention, and learning from him at every opportunity I had. My mindset was simple. If Ryan stayed late, I stayed late. Some nights we worked until five in the morning to finish projects. I was not chasing work-life balance; I was chasing faithfulness and excellence. When you are building something, you do what it takes. Ryan would often tell me, "Write cheques that scare you, cheques that require faith and God's involvement. Do not rely only on yourself." That principle pushed me to trust God more deeply, because I knew my ability had limits, but His did not. Ryan would also say, "Take care of God's house and He will take care of yours." I held on to that. Over and over, I saw it play out in my life. As I put time, energy, and money into building God's house, He made sure to take care of us and our needs.

Being uncomfortable for a season, along with growth in my business, positioned us to purchase another property the following year. We did whatever we had to do to keep moving forward, and we refused to let issues stop us. Even in the middle of those uncomfortable choices, God was faithful. Every time we sacrificed to put

His house first, He took care of our needs. He always provided a way forward, often in ways that were extraordinary for our age.

One pivotal moment came during a late-night conversation with Troy. He said, "Most people will settle for mediocrity because they're not willing to bear the struggle of success. They don't want to be crushed, and therefore they won't ever find out their true potential." Then he asked me, "So are you willing to bear the pain?" I replied yes, and he replied, "Then get ready to be crushed." I walked away convinced that extraordinary results require extraordinary decisions and sacrifices. That night, I also realised something important. We are all exactly where we are in life because of the choices we've made, good or bad. If you want things to change, then you have to change what you do, how you live, and who you surround yourself with.

We could have chosen to live a mediocre life, making no changes, and it would not have been a bad life. However, we would have never reached new heights or come across the opportunities God placed in front of us. We would not have been the stewards who multiplied what was entrusted to us. That kind of mediocrity would never have enabled us to serve our mission to be kingdom builders.

That perspective encouraged Nicole and me to change the way we approached everything in our lives, the way we talked about finances, wealth, and budgeting, and the way we made decisions. We decided to grow together and change the input going into our lives. That meant being intentional with the information we consumed, the people we were listening to, and especially the things we talked and dreamed about. It was not just about cutting out the wrong things; it was about filling our minds and hearts with the right ones.

What I was learning in that season reminded me of the parable of the talents in Matthew 25. The wicked servant buried what he was given out of fear, but the faithful ones worked, multiplied, and were entrusted with more. Jesus said, "You have been faithful with little, I will set you over much" (Matthew 25:23). That became my guiding principle. Everything I have belongs to God. I am not the owner, I am a steward. God gives prosperity, and it can be taken away in a moment if it is mismanaged. "Take the talent from him" is the warning to the wicked and lazy servant in Matthew 25:28. God is wise. He cuts off branches that do not bear fruit and prunes fruitful branches so they can bear more fruit (John 15:2). There is no room for laziness or entitlement. God gives and God takes away, and it is only by His mercy that we can accomplish anything worthy.

A significant part of stewardship of finances is tithing. Before Nicole and I were even married, we committed to honouring God with our first fruits by tithing through our local church. I cannot stress this enough. Tithing is one of the clearest ways to start being a good steward and not fall into greed. It shows God that you are submitted to Him with your finances, whether you have a lot or a little. It is simple: if you do not tithe, you are the wicked servant, and what you have will be taken from you and given to the good and faithful servant. God is merciful, but He is also just. Malachi 3 makes it clear. Withholding the tithe is robbing God. People often quote, "If I will not open the windows of heaven for you and pour down for you a blessing until there is no more need" in verse 10, but they overlook verses 8 and 9, where God says, "Will man rob God? Yet you are robbing me. But you say, 'How have we robbed you?' In your tithes and contributions. You are cursed with a curse, for you are robbing me, the whole nation of you."

And God does not just give a command, He gives promises to those who honour Him this way. In Malachi 3:10-12, He says He will open the windows of heaven and pour out a blessing until there is no more need. That is an abundance that cannot be measured. He promises to rebuke the devourer so that what you have is not eaten up, your efforts will not be destroyed, and your fruit will last. And He promises that all nations will see and call you blessed, because your life will reflect His favour in a way that is obvious to the world.

But we cannot make tithing about ourselves. It is not a formula or a deal with God. The tithe is not for our benefit first; it is a praise to God. It is reverence, worship, and obedience. It is declaring that all we have belongs to Him and we are only stewards. Paul wrote, "Whoever sows sparingly will also reap sparingly, and whoever sows generously will also reap generously... for God loves a cheerful giver" (2 Corinthians 9:6-7). If you are tithing, that is just a start, and I would encourage you to grow into giving over and above to meet the needs of the house. As Lee Domingue says, "The pastor determines the vision, but we determine the pace." Real prosperity is not just personal wealth. It is the ability to bless others financially and to serve a great mission, building God's house.

Nicole and I never wanted to wait until we had "made it" to start blessing the church. If we had waited, we would still not be serving our mission to be kingdom builders. Even though I have not made it yet, I am committed to building God's house at whatever stage I am in and at whatever level of wealth Nicole and I possess. Doing the uncomfortable things like moving, downsizing, long hours, and sacrifice positioned us to bless the church financially in our twenties, and I know this is not the end. Through all of it, God has continued to prove Himself faithful, providing opportunities, solutions, and blessings that are far beyond what we should have had at our age.

I am still running my race and asking God for His mercy daily, that I could be a faithful servant and a good steward. My prayer is that He would continue to trust me and you with more, expanding our territories beyond what we can ask or imagine, as we keep building His house.

—Anuar

QUESTIONS FOR REFLECTION

1. Do you believe it is God's will that you prosper in every area of life? Why or why not? What does "prosper" mean to you?

2. What financial mindsets have you inherited from your family and what mindsets must you change?

3. Do you currently practise the principle of tithing to your local church? How have you seen God provide for you?

4. What are your financial goals for the next year, the next five years, and over the course of your life?

5. What is the hardest principle for you to apply from this chapter? What is one small step you could take to begin putting that truth into practice?

NOTES

CHOICE 8

DISCIPLINES

Every dream in your heart is built with good disciplines.

MY STORY

When I was twenty-two years old, I was invited to be the youth pastor of a church in Moose Jaw, Saskatchewan. When the pastor was giving me direction regarding my job description, I said, "Pastor, would it be acceptable to you if I spend the first hour at work reading the Bible and praying?" He reluctantly agreed, and so I established my life on one hour of prayer and reading the Word of God. This hour of prayer would shape the destiny of my life and become a practice through many seasons as I have taken leadership in God's great church.

After working in the church for about six months and practicing this discipline of one hour in the Word of God and prayer at the beginning of my workday, I experienced something unforgettable. Suddenly, an inner voice spoke to me with very clear words: "Mel, you will be moving to Vancouver, and you will be the youth pastor of the Evangelistic Tabernacle."

The directive was so clear that at the end of the day, I drove to my fiancée's house and said to Heather, "We will be moving to Vancouver and will become the youth pastors of the Evangelistic Tabernacle."

She said, "Oh, really?"

The good news is that when God speaks a word of direction to you and informs you of His will for your life, His word to you will be confirmed and will come to pass.

I had never attended the church in Vancouver before and had no previous contact with Pastor J. Phillip Johnson, but somehow word of us had reached him, and he felt impressed upon to invite us to become the youth pastors of the great church he was leading. Within ten days I received a letter in the mail inviting us to move to Vancouver and become the youth pastors.

It was during our first year of marriage in Vancouver that we experienced a renewal of the Holy Spirit, learned how to lead a church, and connected with the Jesus Revolution movement that would set us up for the future, preparing Heather and I to plant Home Church in Red Deer.

God has big plans that He wants to share with you when you establish a disciplined life in the Word and in prayer.

Setting this foundation of discipline established my relationship with God so I could hear God's voice and do His will. It was not just discipline for discipline's sake, but discipline so I could live an orderly life and establish my future. And discipline will do the same for you!

THE FOUNDATION OF DISCIPLINES

Spiritual disciplines are the foundation that shapes your entire future. The Bible says, "Be diligent to present yourself approved to God, a worker who does not need to be ashamed, rightly dividing the word of truth." This is not a suggestion. It's a blueprint for spiritual success.

It's important to realise that there's a vast difference between knowing you should read your Bible and actually developing the discipline to do it consistently. It's like the difference between owning exercise equipment and using it regularly. The equipment alone doesn't make you healthy—the discipline of using it does.

Joshua 1:8 gives us God's formula for success: meditate on His Word, day and night. Not just read it—meditate on it. Let it sink deep into your spirit. I've watched countless young people transform their lives by simply establishing this one discipline. It's a matter of consistency.

Jesus told a story about two builders. Both faced the same storms, the same challenges, the same pressures. But one built on rock, while the other chose sand. The difference wasn't in the quality of their buildings—it was in their foundation.

Life will test every one of us. Too many people who thought they could skip the disciplines of Bible study, prayer, and meditation find their lives crumbling when storms hit. The time to build your foundation is before the storm, not during the storm.

SCRIPTURES ABOUT DISCIPLINES

Hebrews 12:11 (TPT)
"Now all discipline seems to be painful at the time, yet later it will produce a transformation of character, bringing a harvest of righteousness and peace to those who yield to it."

Proverbs 13:4 (NASB)
"The soul of the lazy one craves and gets nothing, But the soul of the diligent is made prosperous."

Timothy 4:7–8 (NIV)
"Train yourself to be godly. For physical training is of some value, but godliness has value for all things, holding promise for both the present life and the life to come."

Proverbs 25:28 (NIV)
"Like a city whose walls are broken through is a person who lacks self-control."

Titus 2:11–12 (NIV)
"For the grace of God has appeared that offers salvation to all people. It teaches us to say 'No' to ungodliness and worldly passions, and to live self-controlled, upright and godly lives in this present age."

JUSTICE'S STORY

Hi, my name is Justice Sebastian, from the Philippines. My grandmother is Bishop Vicky Sebastian, and my parents are Pastor Joshua Sebastian and Sister Giselle Sebastian.

I accepted Jesus Christ in my heart when I was four years old. Back then, I made a decision to be a disciplined follower of Jesus Christ and read the Bible, because in there I find all of God's great plans and promises for my life. An example is Jeremiah 29:11, which clearly states that God's plan for our lives is for us to prosper and to live to the fullest.

The Bible is important and needs to be read every day to keep you strong, so that you can stay deeply rooted in God's Word and resist the temptations of the devil and all the challenges and trials you may face in this imperfect and fallen world. It is important to have a disciplined life, because God will use you as His instrument to shine His light through you to other people around you who are still living in the darkness and do not know Jesus Christ and His great sacrifice.

—Justice

THE POWER OF A DISCIPLINED LIFE

When my son Jachin was fourteen, he made a decision that would shape his entire future. He bought a Bible reading plan called Bedroom Bible College and committed himself to daily reading and meditation. As I watched him develop this discipline, I saw remarkable growth. Today, he pastors Home Church, a leading church in Canada—and it all started with those teenage disciplines.

Let me outline the essential disciplines that will help you build on solid ground. These are things that have given me success in my own experience, and I've seen them work in many other people as well.

1.   Read and study the Bible.

The Bible might seem intimidating at first, but it's actually much easier to understand than you might realise. One of the biggest keys is to understand that it is actually made up of sixty-six small books. Each book is different, and once you start to learn what they are about, you'll be able to find encouragement and teaching for your daily life.

- *Start with a simple reading plan.* You can find one online, or there are Bible reading apps such as YouVersion (also called the Bible App).

- *Take notes and mark key verses that speak to you*. Nobody is grading you here. Just write down things God speaks to you.

- *Meditate on Scripture*. "Meditation" means thinking something over for a while. This is about letting God's Word saturate your thinking. When I counsel young ministers, I often ask them, "What verse are you currently meditating on?" The answers tell me a lot about their spiritual health.

- *Memorize key passages.* In my early ministry years, I made a commitment to memorize verses daily. Those verses became anchors during difficult times. They're like spiritual ammunition—you never know when you'll need them, but when you do, you'll be grateful they're there.

- *Practise obedience.* James tells us to "be doers of the word, and not hearers only, deceiving yourselves" (James 1:22 NKJV). This is where many stumble. They know what to do but lack the discipline to do it. What I've learned is that delayed obedience is really just disobedience. When God speaks through His Word, act on it immediately.

2. Establish prayer rhythms.

Those morning prayer times I told you about weren't always comfortable or convenient. But they became the heartbeat of my ministry. Prayer doesn't have to be complicated. It's simply talking with God and learning to hear His voice. The more consistently you pray, the more natural it becomes.

- *Set a daily time to pray.* Maybe it's early morning, lunch break, or evening. It doesn't have to be long—start with five or ten minutes. Consistency matters more than length.

- *Keep it simple and honest.* You don't need fancy words. Just talk to God about what's happening in your life, what you're worried about, and what you're grateful for.

- *Use the Lord's Prayer as a guide.* Jesus gave us a pattern in Matthew 6: praise God, pray for His will, ask for your needs, seek forgiveness, and ask for strength against temptation.

- *Listen as much as you speak.* Prayer is a conversation. After you pray, take a moment to be still. Often God speaks through peace, clarity, or a quiet inner prompting aligned with Scripture.

- *Pray throughout the day.* Whisper quick prayers as you work, drive, study, or walk. Scripture says, "pray without ceasing" (1 Thessalonians 5:17 NKJV), which means staying connected to God moment by moment.

- *Keep a simple prayer list.* Write down people or situations you're praying for. When God answers, mark it down and let it build your faith.

3. Maintain order in your personal space.

There's often a strong connection between the condition of your physical space and the condition of your inner life. When everything around you is messy and chaotic, it's hard to stay focused, calm, or spiritually grounded.

The Bible says, "Let all things be done decently and in order" (1 Corinthians 14:40 NKJV). Paul was talking about church services, but it's a healthy pattern for your whole life. For example:

- *Make your bed every morning.* It sets the tone for the day and gives your mind a small win right away.

- *Keep your room clean and picked up.* Aim for a weekly reset, if not a daily one. For most of us, a clear space can help create a clear mind.

- *Organize your study or work area.* When your environment is in order, it's much easier to concentrate on your prayer and Bible reading time, which means it will be easier to hear from God.

- *Take responsibility for your space.* Make your space a place you like to be, where you feel safe and at rest. Don't wait until things are out of control. Small, consistent effort builds discipline.

Through the years, I've watched many young people struggle spiritually while their living spaces looked like disaster zones. If you bring order to your external world, it gets much easier to bring order to your internal world as well.

4. Manage your finances with intention.

Few areas reveal our discipline level like how we handle money. Proverbs 27:23 instructs us to "know well the condition of your flocks, and pay attention to your herds." In modern terms: know your financial situation and manage it deliberately. The disciplines you establish now will determine your financial future for decades to come.

- *Keep track of what you spend.* I remember when Heather and I were first married. We had very little, but we established the discipline of tracking every dollar. We used a simple budget system with envelopes—one for tithe, one for rent, one for groceries, one for savings, and so on. This basic discipline protected us from the financial chaos that destroys many young marriages. Start by tracking everything you spend for one month. Then create a simple budget. Save something, even if it's just $10 a week. Pay your bills on time. Know where your money is going, how much you have left, and what you need to save for.

- *Master the art of delayed gratification.* In a world of one-click purchases and buy-now-pay-later options, the discipline of waiting has nearly vanished. Yet Proverbs repeatedly warns about hasty financial decisions. I've watched young people destroy their financial future by surrendering to immediate desires rather than practicing patience. Start by implementing the 48-hour rule for any non-essential purchase over $50. Wait two days before buying. You'll be amazed how many "must-haves" become "can-waits" when you exercise this simple discipline.

- *Establish the habit of giving first.* When I counsel young adults about finances, I often hear, "I'll start tithing when I make more money." This backwards thinking misses the powerful principle Jesus taught: "Where your treasure is, there your heart will be also" (Matthew 6:21 NKJV). Begin now, with whatever you have. The discipline of giving first —before paying bills, before entertainment, before savings—establishes a foundation of stewardship that will serve you for life. I've never met a consistent tither who regretted this discipline.

- *Develop a practice of consistent saving.* Proverbs 21:20 tells us, "In the house of the wise are stores of choice food and oil, but a foolish man devours all he has (NIV)." The discipline of saving isn't just about accumulating money—it's about developing the character qualities of discipline and self-control. Start with an emergency fund, even if it's just $25 per paycheck. The amount matters less than the habit. This discipline builds financial resilience that will help protect you when life's inevitable storms arrive.

- *Gain knowledge and financial wisdom.* Too many Christians ignore financial responsibility, thinking money matters are somehow unspiritual. Yet Proverbs 24:3-4 tells us, "By wisdom a house is built, and through understanding it is established; through knowledge its rooms are filled with rare and beautiful treasures" (NIV). Learn what you can about budgeting, negotiating, time management, savings, investments, buying a home, and any other area where you need to grow. There is always more to learn, and information is readily available if you're willing to put in the effort. Read books, listen to podcasts, take a class, watch videos. The discipline of financial education will compound throughout your lifetime.

- *Be content.* Paul writes in Philippians 4:12, "I have learned the secret of being content in any and every situation" (NIV). Note the word "learned" here. Contentment is a discipline that must be developed. In a culture constantly telling you that you need more, the ability to say "I have enough" is revolutionary. Start by practicing gratitude daily for what you already have. Compare yourself to God's Word, not to Instagram influencers. The discipline of contentment will free you from the treadmill of materialism that traps so many young adults.

5. Invest in your physical health.

Your body is a temple of the Holy Spirit. Scripture reminds us of this: "Do you not know that your bodies are temples of the Holy Spirit, who is in you, whom you have received from God? You are not your own; you were bought at a price. Therefore honour God with your bodies" (1 Corinthians 6:19–20 NIV). Your body belongs to God, not you. How are you stewarding what He has entrusted to you? Here are some simple, practical habits that build discipline:

- *Get consistent sleep*. A rested body thinks clearer, prays clearer, and stays spiritually alert.

- *Eat nutritious food*. Fuel matters. The way you feed your body often shapes the way you feel and function.

- *Exercise regularly*. You don't need a gym membership—start with walking, stretching, or light workouts. Movement builds energy and mental strength.

- *Stay hydrated*. Drinking more water seems small, but it improves focus, mood, and overall health.

- *Limit what drains you*. Too much sugar, stress, junk food, caffeine, or screen time can steal your energy.

- *Start small and stay consistent*. Healthy habits build discipline, and discipline strengthens every part of your spiritual life.

Through the years, I've watched gifted leaders lose momentum because they ignored their health. You can't run your race well if your body breaks down. Steward your physical life, and your spiritual life will grow stronger too.

GETTING STARTED

Starting these disciplines isn't as complicated as many think. But it does require intentional choices. That first hour I committed to prayer and Bible reading wasn't random. I specifically asked my mentor, "Pastor, would it be acceptable that I spend the first hour of my working day between 9 and 10 am in the reading of the Word and prayer?" You need that kind of planned, specific commitment.

The most important thing is to keep at it. Disciplines don't produce dramatic results every day. They are small, unseen acts that add up to a transformed lifestyle. Every morning, you make a choice. When that alarm goes off, you're choosing between discipline and distraction. I've watched too many promising ministries fade because people choose comfort over consistency.

Remember what Jesus said about the wise and foolish builders? Both faced the same storms. The only difference was their foundation. Every day you choose spiritual disciplines, you're building your house upon the rock of God's Word.

As you learn and grow in these disciplines, find the tools that work for you. Just as my son Jachin found Bedroom Bible College, you need to find tools that work for your learning style and schedule. Maybe it's a Bible app, a journal, or a reading plan. The key is finding what helps you maintain consistency.

When it comes to your time with God, it's helpful to have a "sacred space," a place where you consistently seek Him. It might be a corner of your bedroom, a desk, or even your car during lunch break. Find a time and place when you can leave the pressure of the day behind and focus on God.

Now, let me challenge you directly. What specific time will you set aside for God's Word and prayer? Not a vague "sometime," but a specific appointment. Write it down. Tell someone who'll hold you accountable.

And beyond spiritual disciplines, what practical steps will you take towards financial order? Will you commit to tracking expenses, creating a budget, saving consistently? Will you exercise discipline in your body, your health, your room, your schedule, your car, your free time? These seemingly small decisions will shape your future in ways you can't yet imagine.

Years from now, someone might ask you, like they ask me, "How did it all begin?" Will you be able to point back to the disciplines you established today? Will you have a story like my son Jachin's, where teenage commitments laid the groundwork for pastoral leadership?

Every great move of God I've witnessed began with someone's personal discipline. Someone who chose to pray when others slept. Someone who studied when others played. Someone who managed their finances wisely when others spent carelessly. Someone who persevered when others quit.

The question isn't whether God wants to use you. He does. The question is whether you'll develop the disciplines that position you to be used, because the foundation you build today determines what God can build through you tomorrow. Will you be like young Joseph, maintaining your integrity even when no one's watching? Or like Daniel, establishing prayer patterns that withstand even royal decrees? The choice is yours.

KENDRICK'S STORY

Growing up in the church, especially with a mom who worked on staff, I was taught early on that church was non-negotiable. If the doors were open, my family was there. Looking back, I realise that a seed of discipline was planted in me from a young age.

But just showing up to church doesn't automatically mean you're living as a disciple of Jesus. Being physically present is one thing, but building a personal relationship with Jesus is something else entirely. That depth of relationship is a personal choice, and how far it goes is completely up to you.

Being in church for so long, I've had the privilege of watching many different people live out their faith. I noticed something consistent: the people who truly lived a "God-first" life—those who were in the Word daily, faithfully attended church, tithed, and worshipped wholeheartedly—bore real, lasting fruit in their lives. In contrast, those who were present but didn't live with intentionality often lacked that same fruitfulness.

Seeing this made it clear to me: if I wanted to live a life that produces fruit, I needed to start living with more discipline.

The first area I really committed to was tithing. From the moment I received my first paycheck, I decided that God would get the first 10 percent. There were a few times when I forgot or got off track, and each time, it felt like my life would start to unravel. I'd fall behind in school or face unexpected challenges. Those experiences taught me quickly that when I align my finances with God's principles, I experience peace and order in my life.

The next area I focused on was my Bible reading. I had always wanted to be consistent, but it never became a true daily habit until a guest speaker came to our church and talked about the power of just two simple disciplines: daily Bible reading and daily prayer. He shared story after story of how those habits transformed people's lives. That word really stuck with me, and I made the decision right then to commit. That year, for the first time in my life, I read my Bible every single day.

I truly believe that God has incredible things in store for each of us. He wants to be in close relationship with us, but that takes intentional effort on our part—time spent learning who He is and *how He designed us to live. The Bible says, "Draw near to God, and He will draw near to you." That promise is real.*

Many people think that living a disciplined life is restrictive, or even punishing. But I've found the opposite to be true. Living with discipline actually opens you up to the fullness *of what God has for you. It fills you with His Word so that it can overflow out of you. Not just for your own benefit, but to bless others too.*

Practically, that's looked like waking up early enough to spend time in the Word, or if I missed it in the morning, making sure I found time later in the day before bed. Discipline started for me with understanding my total dependence on God.

A couple of years ago, I went through a really difficult season mentally. I was struggling just to get out of bed. It was in that season that I learned how to fully rely on God for strength. I poured out my heart to Him, and in that desperation, I developed a hunger for His presence and His Word because it was the only thing keeping me going.

Coming out of that time, I understood more deeply how essential *it is to stay in His presence and keep His Word in your heart. When life gets hard—and it will—it's that foundation that gives you the strength and wisdom to keep moving forward.*

Don't hold back from the life God has for you. Living a disciplined life isn't always easy, and I still have moments where I mess up. But I've seen over and over again that this is the best way to stay close to God and walk in everything He has for me.

—Kendrick

QUESTIONS FOR REFLECTION

1. Do you have a Bible reading plan? If not, what simple plan could you commit to starting tomorrow?

2. When and where will you have your daily "appointment with God"? What specific time and place will you designate for prayer and Bible study?

3. What areas of your financial life need more discipline right now? Are you tracking expenses? Do you have a budget? Are you saving consistently?

4. Look at your physical environment (your room, car, workspace). What does the order or disorder of these spaces reveal about your inner life? What one area could you bring more order to this week?

5. What one discipline—spiritual, financial, or personal—if consistently practiced for the next year, would most dramatically transform your life? What's your plan to develop this discipline?

NOTES

CHOICE 9
CONFIDENCE

Confidence is built one step at a time.

"For this reason I remind you to fan into flame the gift of God,
which is in you through the laying on of my hands."
(2 Timothy 1:6 NIV)

MY STORY

When I was 32 years old, I received a terrible phone call from my sister Sharon. She said, "I have some very bad news. Dad has hung himself with a rope." I was devastated, and I was also angry that my father, at age sixty-two, would take his life, leaving behind my mother, my siblings, and my two children, Christy and Jachin, without a grandfather.

I gathered my siblings together. A leader in the church lent us his beautiful blue Ford Mercury to make the trip to bury my father. With four in the front and four in the back of the car, we began our journey to my father's funeral in Victoria, BC. Sitting in the back of the car, I began speaking to my siblings as we began our trip through the beautiful Rocky Mountains in Rogers Pass. I began venting my anger about what dad had done, not only to himself but to his family.

Then I began saying to my siblings, "Unfortunately, I'm just like Dad. The Bible says that the sins of the fathers are visited to the third and fourth generation. I am a chip off the old block—what is in Dad is in me."

But as we drove and talked, I was reminded of a powerful truth that changed everything. The sins in my family tree did not need to pass on to me because there is another tree—the Cross of Calvary.

That day, as we drove through the bridges climbing up the huge mountain passes, I asked God to deliver me. I prayed, "God, deliver me from the sins that are in my family tree." And suddenly I felt a release, and God set me free.

I found myself free, but empty inside. God's design for developing confidence in young people is meant to flow through mentoring, especially from father to son. Though my father was a good man, he never learned how to build close relationships with his sons. Without that crucial connection and his guidance to build my confidence, I grew up wrestling with deep insecurity.

When I returned from the funeral, I realised I had to develop my identity as a man and fill my life with confidence. That would take place by two important actions: the choosing of mentors to fill my life with what I had not received from my father, and confidence that came from confessing the Word of God. I took Scriptures and placed them on cards, and on the back of the cards, I wrote positive statements. I would pull the cards out of my pocket daily and confess the Word of God.

Through that experience, I put together 31 confessions that I read on a regular basis. These confessions became the foundation of my book *Be A Man*. I have included them at the back of this book for you. I encourage you to read them daily, as I did, and watch what God will do.

It took me a while to change my flawed thinking. It was an intentional process. But I was encouraged when I realised some of the Bible's greatest leaders had to change their faulty thinking too.

Gideon was hiding in a wine press, where no one would see him, threshing out the grain. He and the entire nation were trying to survive for fear of the Philistines who would swoop in and steal their grain and leave the people in poverty. Then an angel appeared to him and said, "You are a mighty man of God." Gideon had to go through the process of changing this thinking about himself, then he led the children of Israel to a great victory (Judges 6-8).

Moses was insecure when God met him at the burning bush and called him to lead the children of Israel out of Egypt and to the Promised Land. He had been raised and educated in Pharaoh's court, but he had to flee for his life. After forty years in the desert, insecurity had become ingrained in his heart, and he suffered from a serious inferiority complex. When God met him in the wilderness, he had lost his ability to speak confidently.

Timothy lacked confidence when the Apostle Paul was sending him as a young leader to become the bishop of Ephesus, the largest church in the world at that time. It was a challenging opportunity that brought out his insecurity. So Paul wrote to him: "For God has not given us a spirit of fear, but of power and of love and of a sound mind" (2 Timothy 1:7 NKJV).

Our confidence is always challenged when God asks us to do greater things that we feel we are capable of doing. It's a battle we all must fight—to stop listening to the voices of fear, limitation, and inadequacy, and to replace them with a bold, faith-inspired view of ourselves that is based on God's limitless thoughts towards us.

CALLING AND CONFIDENCE

The kind of confidence that comes from knowing who you are in Christ is not the same thing as the arrogance that comes from pride, comparison, or looking down on others.

Godly confidence comes from knowing your identity and purpose in Jesus. It's the quiet, steady assurance that God created you on purpose and for a purpose. It doesn't make you boastful or self-focused. Instead, it gives you the courage to step into what God has called you to do, while keeping a humble heart.

Arrogance, on the other hand, is when you start measuring yourself against other people. It shows up as pride, comparison, or feeling like you're better than someone else. That attitude has nothing to do with the confidence God wants for you. In fact, arrogance is the opposite of the security we have in Christ.

Godly confidence lifts others up. Arrogance pushes others down. One comes from knowing who you are in Jesus; the other comes from trying to prove who you are without Him.

CONFIDENCE WHEN YOU'RE YOUNG

The best time to start building the kind of confidence that Moses, Jeremiah, and Esther discovered is when you are young. I believe every young person needs confidence, now more than ever.

Your teenage years are a time when you're figuring out who you are. You're discovering your personality, your strengths, and the purpose God has put inside you. Developing confidence helps you anchor your identity in those God-given qualities instead of in other people's opinions.

These years also come with challenges, transitions, and emotions that can feel overwhelming at times. And your hormones aren't helping you out very much, either. But confidence gives you the strength to bounce back when life hits hard. It helps you handle stress and push through obstacles.

Studies show that confident young people set bigger goals, and they actually pursue them. Confidence gives you the motivation and discipline you need to chase the dreams God has placed in your heart.

Confidence also affects your relationships. It helps you interact with friends, teachers, parents, and even romantic interests in a healthy way. When you're confident, you're better at setting boundaries, communicating clearly, avoiding wrong relationships, and making good decisions even in the face of peer pressure.

When you're confident, you're also more likely to step up as a leader—in school, at church, on a team, or in your family. You become someone who influences the people around you for good. Confidence keeps you from shrinking back or staying silent when you should speak up. It helps you try new things and grow past your comfort zone.

Ultimately, confidence gives you the strength you need to navigate these important years with wisdom. As you learn to walk confidently in who you are in Jesus, you'll be able to live with purpose and influence—just like the biblical heroes who inspire us.

JASMIN'S STORY
Turkey

Hello, my name is Jasmin! I am half Russian and half Georgian. Although I was born in Russia, I grew up in Turkey.

I grew up in a Christian family, and even before I was born, I was dedicated to God. I believe that strongly influenced my life and my choices. From the very beginning, my parents would tell me about God and Jesus Christ. We prayed together and read the Bible, and at the age of seventeen, I was baptized and accepted Jesus Christ as my Lord.

A couple years ago. My family and I faced a very difficult time. We had serious financial struggles, housing issues with threats of eviction, and food shortages—all of which affected our health.

In the summer of 2023, our perfectly healthy dog suddenly died in one day after eating something off the street. Losing him so unexpectedly was deeply painful for me. I started having serious health issues—I constantly felt nauseous and I could only eat one spoonful of porridge a day—sometimes not even that. I lost fourteen kilograms in just two weeks.

At that time, I didn't receive the support I had expected from the people I thought would. I felt empty, and because of total exhaustion, fear, and anxiety, I began to drift away from God. I started having panic attacks. Fear and doubt consumed me. I lost the desire to live. I saw no meaning in life.

Thank God for my parents, even when I pushed them away, they patiently continued to support me and helped me—with God's help—to overcome my fears. I couldn't have done it alone. Listening to them, I started praying and asking God to give me victory over my fears. It wasn't easy. Even praying felt hard. But I believed that with God, anything is possible.

By faith, I began stepping out of my comfort zone, which had become my bedroom—I hardly ever left because of the anxiety. I started to go to Home Church and was welcomed so warmly, it was as if they had been waiting for me. That meant so much.

Recovery was slow and difficult. But I kept moving forward, and God helped me overcome all my fears! I am no longer afraid of the things that used to paralyze me. Those things no longer control me. He healed me, and today I am a different person from the one who was consumed with doubt and fear.

I could have never done it without God, all glory and praise to Him!

—Jazmin

SCRIPTURES ABOUT CONFIDENCE

Philippians 1:6 (NLT)
"And I am certain that God, who began the good work within you, will continue his work until it is finally finished on the day when Christ Jesus returns."

Psalm 27:3 (NLT)
"Though a mighty army surrounds me, my heart will not be afraid. Even if I am attacked, I will remain confident."

Proverbs 3:26 (NIV)
"For the Lord will be your confidence and will keep your foot from being caught."

Hebrews 10:35 (NLT)
"So do not throw away this confident trust in the Lord. Remember the great reward it brings you!"

Jeremiah 17:7 (NIV)
"But blessed is the one who trusts in the Lord, whose confidence is in him."

1 John 5:14 (NIV)
"This is the confidence we have in approaching God: that if we ask anything according to his will, he hears us."

Psalm 118:6 (NLT)
"The Lord is for me, so I will have no fear. What can mere people do to me?"

GROWING IN CONFIDENCE

We've established we need confidence. But how do you actually get it? Here are six practical ways you can grow in godly, Jesus-centred confidence.

1. Root your identity in Christ.

I have never forgotten my humble beginnings. But more importantly, I have tried to never forget the greatness of our God and who I am in Him. To be confident, we must remember that our worth, security, and standing before God come from our position as His beloved children, not from our own merits (Ephesians 1:3–6). When we try new things or make mistakes along the way, we can be confident because we know God is with us and He strengthens us.

2. Trust in God's sovereignty and promises.

As we've seen already, God has a plan for our lives, and His plans for us are good. We can rest in the knowledge that He is in control, working all things together for our good (Romans 8:28). We can cling to God's unfailing Word and the certainty of His faithful character (2 Timothy 3:16–17, Hebrews 13:5–6). This means even when things seem dark or uncertain, we can face the future with confidence.

3. Rely on the Holy Spirit's power.

One of the greatest ways we can approach every situation in life is by acknowledging the Holy Spirit's strength in our weaknesses (2 Corinthians 12:9–10). When we remember that we have the third person of the Trinity living in us, working in us to bring God's plans to fulfilment, we have a confidence we could never have on our own.

4.   Serve others humbly and sacrificially.

Often the best thing you can do to grow in confidence is to use your God-given gifts and talents to bless others (1 Peter 4:10–11). My son Jachin preached a powerful message once reminding us that our purpose as followers of Jesus is people. Nothing fuels us like making a difference in the lives of those God puts in our path.

5.   Renew your mind regularly.

As a pastor, I have often taught about the importance of renewing our minds and changing the way we think. The key to doing this lies in meditating on God's Word, which has the power to transform our thought patterns and fill us with hope (Romans 12:1–2, Philippians 4:8).

6.   Surround yourself with people who can encourage and challenge you.

Being in a community with fellow believers who can encourage, challenge, and spur you on is also crucial (Hebrews 10:24–25). The church plays an important role in reminding us of the truth of God's word and helping us combat the lies and insecurities that so often plague us.

It's no secret that the world is constantly trying to squeeze you into its mold. Everywhere you look, you see people struggling with insecurity, trying to find their place and identity. That's why it's so important to let God's Word shape you from the inside out.

As a young person, you need to understand something: insecurity will always try to creep in. Problems, setbacks, mistakes, and fear will try to convince you that you're not enough. Negative voices—online, at school, sometimes even in your own head—will try to pull you down. Every day, you'll have a choice to make: will you give in to the discouraging messages around you, or will you choose to walk confidently in who God says you are?

The road to real, lasting confidence isn't always easy, but it's absolutely worth it. As you walk this journey, you'll discover that God-given courage and Spirit-led creativity will carry you. They will give you the strength you need to live out your identity in Christ, no matter what situation or circumstances you find yourself in.

DAKOTA' STORY

Hey, young person. My name is Dakota, but you can call me Kota. I'm an 18-year-old kid from Hawaii. I'm a pastor's kid who grew up in the church.

I want to start by saying that I'm glad you're reading this. Whether your pastor or best friend pushed this into your hands, or whether you're personally hungry for change and growth, we all start somewhere. My desire is that the words that follow would impact you eternally.

You'd be surprised how little being a pastor's kid matters when it comes to having a relationship with the Lord. At some point, I had to face the fact that my parents couldn't have a relationship with God on my behalf. Somewhere along the way, I convinced myself that God was either completely fake, or that He existed but disliked me in particular. I couldn't "feel" God, and it seemed like everyone around me was faking it. So instead of chasing Him, I chased satisfaction in worldly things. I chased every desire, every temptation, every emotion, every worthless thing that temporarily filled the void in my heart—when in reality, that void was made to be filled by Jesus.

On paper, I had everything going for me. I can play seven different instruments, I've always been creative and athletic, and I can figure almost anything out if I put my mind to it. I would have been great at anything that I wanted to do, but even with all of that ability, I felt incredibly lost. Something was missing. Nothing felt right.

That all changed when I was 15. My entire life flipped upside down the day I had a radical encounter with Jesus Christ. I went to a youth camp and told myself, "If I don't experience God here, I'm going to stop pretending he exists." Something you'll learn about me is that I don't play pretend. Beneath all the anger and fear was a heart that longed for a real relationship with the Creator of the universe.

And that's exactly what I found. In the moment He met me, I knew—without a doubt—that He was real. Not just real, but personal. Everything began to fall into place. I started to understand God's character and believe that what He says is true.

Some time later, Pastor Mel asked me, "Do you have any doubts? What do you have doubts about?" I told him, "It would be faster for me to tell you what I don't have doubts about." Even though I knew God was real, I didn't yet know much about who He was. Pastor Mel encouraged me to write down my doubts and then go through each one, asking the question: "What does the Bible say about your doubts?"

So I did. One verse that changed everything for me was Jeremiah 29:11: "For I know the plans I have for you," declares the Lord, "plans to prosper you and not to harm you, plans to give you hope and a future." I found that to be true in my own life. Another scripture that became real to me was Proverbs 3:5-6: "Trust in the

Lord with all your heart and lean not on your own understanding; in all your ways acknowledge Him, and He will make your paths straight."

So when Pastor Mel later asked me, "What made you a confident person?" I realised this: I'm not confident because of who I am. My confidence doesn't come from my abilities, my personality, or my talents. None of those ever got me very far. My confidence comes from truly knowing the character of God—that He's true, faithful, loving, and the same yesterday, today, and forever. He has never let me down—and He never will.

Today, I'm proud to serve my church as a youth leader, worship leader, and in so many other ways for the glory of God. But more importantly, I'm proud to live as a full-time imitator of Jesus outside the walls of the church, proclaiming the good news of Christ crucified to anyone who will listen. My life has been irreversibly changed.

My prayer for you, young person, is that you would come to realise the God you serve. Life changes when you understand that the fear of figuring everything out on your own is actually a good thing. You're not meant to do life alone. God has a plan and a destiny for your life, but it's a choice to walk in it. My hope is that you will choose to step into His plans. There is a joy and peace beyond all understanding that fills you when you lean on Him and run to Him in times of need.

What consumes me most is the desperate desire to see people like you walk closely with God in your youth. I wish I had fully served Him with my teenage years, because there's nothing like this life. Maybe you've been unsure. Maybe life has beaten down your confidence in Jesus. But hear me: the first step to experiencing what I've experienced is a relationship with Jesus—not religion, not empty rules, but real relationship.

So how do you have a relationship with Jesus? The first step is to be in right standing with God, or as Christians call it: salvation.

Romans 10:9-10 says, "If you confess with your mouth that

Jesus is Lord and believe in your heart that God raised Him from the dead, you will be saved. For with the heart one believes and is justified, and with the mouth one confesses and is saved."

So it starts with confessing and believing. But relationship doesn't end at salvation—it begins there. James 4:8 says, "Draw near to God, and He will draw near to you.". Practically, you can draw near to Him by reading your Bible, praying, spending time praising and worshipping Him.

As you grow closer to God, your life and the way you live it will begin to change. The Bible says in 1 John 1:7, "If we walk in the light as He is in the light, we have fellowship with one another, and the blood of Jesus His Son cleanses us from all sin." That means when you walk with Jesus, you don't just grow in your relationship with Him—you also grow in your relationships with other believers.

So finally: Surround yourself with godly friends who will encourage you in the Lord and support you in your walk of faith, and don't forget to tell people about how Jesus has affected your life! Your words have the potential to make an eternal difference in someone's life.

May the grace of God be with you, his love surround you, and His joy be your strength.

—Dakota

QUESTIONS FOR REFLECTION

1. On a scale of 1 to 10, how confident are you? Why did you score yourself that way?

2. Are you happy with your overall level of confidence? Why or why not?

3. Are there specific areas in which you lack confidence? What actions could you take to build confidence in those areas?

4. Who are the mentors, leaders, or friends in your life who consistently speak confidence and truth into you? How can you lean into those relationships more intentionally?

NOTES

CHOICE 10
ENJOY LIFE

Choose the "enjoyment of life."

MY STORY

One day in 1974, I walked into the car dealership to purchase a brand-new car. We were pastoring in the "Jesus People" movement at the height of the Jesus revolution, and we were in need of reliable transportation. Our car was at the end of its life, had many dents, and needed to be replaced. It did not represent us or Jesus very well.

An older pastor friend informed me that he had a special relationship with the Plymouth dealership, and we could purchase a brand-new Plymouth Fury at the fleet price: just $4225. His church would make the monthly payment so we could own the vehicle.

Wow! A brand-new car! We were so excited. This was a miracle. As pastors living on a poverty wage, we rejoiced that God was providing the vehicle we needed.

We looked at all the beautiful cars, and I fell in love with one in the showroom: a red-and-white vehicle with white bucket seats, a console in the middle, and windows that opened with the push of a button rather than a window crank handle. I was jumping for joy at the thought that I could have a car like this for just a few dollars more than the other cars.

I said, "Pastor, this is the one I want."

He answered, "Pastors don't drive fancy cars like this." Then he pointed to a dirty-grey-coloured car and said, "Here is the car for you." The seats were grey cloth, the steering wheel wasn't leather, and it was so ugly.

Unfortunately, I gave in to the pressure from the pastor, made a deal, and drove out of the lot with a brand-new, terrible-looking, ugly grey vehicle.

I allowed myself to live less than the better plan. I was thankful that God had provided transportation, but I always asked myself, Why did I settle for less when I could have received something better, along with the enjoyment of life?

This experience taught me a lesson I will never forget. Life is made to be enjoyed. Every purchase that you make in life, the house you live in, the clothes you wear, and the vacations that you take should produce joy and happiness in life.

Why live with second-best when there will be enough tragedy, circumstances, and trials without adding any more negative to life? My philosophy from that day on became "Enjoy Life." Jesus came that you might have life and have it more abundantly (John 10:10).

IF IT AIN'T FUN, IT AIN'T GOD

A lot of young people don't want to serve God or fully surrender to His will because they're convinced God's plan will bring nothing but misery. They've wrongfully been led to believe that serving God means a life of drudgery, doing everything they hate while watching everyone else have fun and adventure. Nothing could be further from the truth! There is no life more exciting than walking with God and doing His will.

Ecclesiastes 8:15 says, "So I commend the enjoyment of life, because there is nothing better for a person under the sun than to eat and drink and be glad. Then joy will accompany them in their toil all the days of the life God has given them under the sun." God created us with both the desire and ability to enjoy life, and it pleases Him when we love the life He has given us.

When God created the world, He said to Adam and Eve, "Enjoy the garden," and only restricted them from one tree. When Moses delivered the people of Israel from Egypt, he took them through the wilderness where there was always "just enough" and promised them they would live in a land of milk and honey, a place of great abundance. God's plan is abundance—do not settle for less than the fullness of life.

Over the course of my life, I've learned to intentionally add fun into every aspect of my life. I'm not talking about shallow self-gratification or chasing worldly pleasures. I'm talking about the deep, lasting enjoyment that comes from walking in God's purposes and finding joy in the many blessings that God gives us along the way.

Many Christians have a wrong idea of what it means to live for God. Some think following Jesus means being miserable all the time or that the more you suffer or give things up, the holier you are. Others have a poverty mindset, believing that if they're struggling or lacking something, it must mean they're "spiritual."

But if you think God is anti-enjoyment or anti-fun, then you haven't really understood who He is yet. Yes, God is holy. Yes, He calls us to sacrifice. But He is also the Creator of joy. He invented humour, designed your ability to laugh, and filled the world with things that bring delight. If God wanted you miserable, why would He design human beings with such a massive capacity for joy? Remember what Jesus said in John 10:10 (NKJV): "I have come that they may have life, and that they may have it more abundantly."

Walking with Jesus should increase your joy, not shrink it. But you have to choose that mindset. If you always look for reasons to be discouraged, anxious, or overwhelmed, this world will give you plenty. But if you intentionally decide to enjoy life, to look for blessings, and to practise gratitude, you'll find reasons to be happy and content.

Now, I'm not pretending everything is easy. Life is hard sometimes, and none of us gets through this world without pain, loss, sadness, or fear. But even when life hurts, we can hold on to the truth that God is still good, that He created us with eternal purpose, and that He is with us.

Here's what I've learned over many years of following Jesus: when you start stepping into your God-given purpose, life becomes incredibly fulfilling. Living with joy is part of living with purpose.

I remember, years ago, sitting down with pastors and presenting my "Enjoy Life" philosophy. I would try to tell them, "God's plan is that you enjoy your life, take family vacations, and develop friendship, love and lasting relationships. If you make life fun, your children will serve the Lord all their days."

Unfortunately, many pastors in those days had poverty mindsets, and often it affected their children. These kids grew up thinking that following Jesus meant poverty, not abundance and blessing, and therefore many of them stopped serving the Lord.

I love to enjoy life with my children and grandchildren. We find ways to take trips, enjoy holidays, and travel the world, and we have learned how to do it at a reasonable price. Life is better when you can choose the enjoyment of life.

HOW CAN YOU ENJOY LIFE MORE?

God's plan for you is a rich, fulfilling life. What can you do to make your life more enjoyable? Here are some key areas you should focus on.

1.   Enjoy your calling

When God finished creation, Genesis 1 tells us He saw that it was "very good!" Can you hear the delight in those words? When you discover what God has uniquely created you to do, you'll find profound fulfilment in walking it out.

2. Enjoy your friendships

I have incredible friends all over the world who mean so much to me. Every time we reunite, even after years apart, we pick up right where we left off. Don't take relationships like these for granted.

3. Enjoy your family.

Whether it's your family of origin or the new family you create, cherish every moment together. God created the family unit, and He loves to bless families who are unified in love and commitment to each other.

4. Enjoy your church.

The body of Christ isn't meant to be a burden. It's meant to be a vibrant, life-giving community. Be an active participant, not just a spectator.

5. Enjoy giving generously.

I've discovered that the greatest joy comes from being generous with people. As you open your hands and heart to give of your time and resources, you'll be amazed at the deep fulfilment you discover.

SCRIPTURES ABOUT ENJOYING LIFE

Psalm 16:11 (NIV)
"You make known to me the path of life; you will fill me with joy in your presence, with eternal pleasures at your right hand."

Psalm 37:4 (NIV)
"Take delight in the Lord, and he will give you the desires of your heart."

Proverbs 17:22 (NIV)
"A cheerful heart is good medicine, but a crushed spirit dries up the bones."

Ecclesiastes 3:12–13 (NIV)
"I know that there is nothing better for people than to be happy and to do good while they live. That each of them may eat and drink, and find satisfaction in all their toil—this is the gift of God."

Nehemiah 8:10 (NIV)
"...the joy of the Lord is your strength."

Philippians 4:4 (NIV)
"Rejoice in the Lord always. I will say it again: Rejoice!"

Romans 14:17 (NIV)
"For the kingdom of God is not a matter of eating and drinking, but of righteousness, peace and joy in the Holy Spirit."

COMPARISON WILL STEAL YOUR JOY

I need to touch on a subject that I see is slowly robbing an entire generation of joy: social media. I'm not saying it's all bad, but I've seen it create some serious problems in people's ability to truly enjoy life.

Here's what I've observed:

- You're constantly seeing others' highlight reels while your normal life feels inadequate in comparison.
- You get caught up chasing likes and follows instead of finding your worth in being God's child.
- Hours slip away scrolling that could be spent actually living.
- Your mind gets filled with messages that directly oppose what God says about you and your purpose.

Social media, like anything else, has its value and can simply be a way of catching up with people or celebrating big moments. But it must be managed, kept in its rightful place, and not allowed to dominate your days. Monitor your time and make adjustments when necessary.

Solomon, the wisest and wealthiest man who ever lived, had it all. Imagine having unlimited resources to pursue anything your heart desired. That was Solomon's life—massive building projects, endless parties, unmatched wealth, and worldwide influence. He began his reign in spectacular fashion by writing Proverbs, building the magnificent temple, uniting the kingdom, and enjoying God's abundant blessings.

But somewhere along the way, Solomon lost his focus. He married foreign women who turned his heart from God, began worshipping their idols, and drifted from his first love. The man who started with such wisdom ended up writing Ecclesiastes, a sobering journal of his realization that all earthly pursuits are meaningless, like chasing after the wind. His choices not only left him spiritually empty but set up the kingdom for division after his death. The once wisest man ended up being someone who failed to make good decisions in the latter part of his life.

Solomon's life teaches us a profound lesson: having everything the world offers doesn't guarantee happiness. In fact, chasing pleasure outside of God's design leads to emptiness. True, lasting enjoyment comes from walking in God's purposes.

God isn't against your happiness. He's not sitting in heaven thinking up ways to make your life miserable. Quite the opposite! He created you with the ability to feel deep joy and delight. But that enjoyment comes from living in alignment with His design, not from chasing counterfeits.

Every morning when you wake up, you have a choice. You can either pursue what the world says will make you happy, or you can choose to embrace the abundant life Jesus offers. One leads to temporary pleasure followed by long-term emptiness; the other leads to lasting joy that nothing can shake.

LIFE IS BETTER WITH GOD

Remember that grey car I drove early in my ministry? For me, buying that car represents believing the lie that following God meant settling for less. But Jesus never called us to a life of less. He called us to abundance.

Life is a precious, sacred gift from your Heavenly Father. It's not meant to be endured like I endured that grey car. It's meant to be embraced fully, lived wholly, enjoyed deeply. Not in a shallow, self-centred way, but in the rich, satisfying way that comes from walking closely with God.

When you really understand this truth, everything changes. You'll stop apologizing for the joy God puts in your heart. You'll quit letting others' poverty mindsets make your choices for you. You'll begin to see that serving God and enjoying life aren't opposites— they're perfectly designed to go together.

So let me challenge you to start living like you believe John 10:10. Pursue your God-given purposes with everything you've got. Make an impact in your sphere of influence. But don't forget to enjoy the journey. Take time to laugh. Create memories. Build relationships. Take advantage of each moment.

When you align your life with God's purposes and learn to enjoy His presence along the way, you'll discover the kind of satisfaction no car, no possession, and no worldly pleasure could ever provide. That's the abundant life Jesus promised. And believe me, it's worth far more than any red Fury with white bucket seats.

PABLO'S STORY

Before I met Christ, I would have considered myself an atheist. I didn't believe in God, and honestly, I didn't think I needed to.

One day when I was 13, I ran into a friend while I was out walking. He invited me to youth group, and I went, mostly because I had nothing better to do that day. I didn't really understand anything they were talking about, but I liked the people. They were friendly, welcoming, and real. So, I kept going back.

For about eight months, I kept attending youth group, even though I told everyone I was an atheist. I'd say things like, "I don't agree with what you're saying, but I like hanging out with you." I didn't realise it then, but God was already working on my heart through the friendships and the love I experienced there.

Then one night, at a youth conference, a friend prayed for me. And in that moment, something changed. I can't fully explain it, but I knew it was real. I felt the presence of God for the first time in my life, and I knew He was with me.

Before that, I carried a lot of guilt—though I didn't even understand why. I just always felt like I was in trouble or doing something wrong. When I encountered Jesus, that guilt lifted. There was peace where there used to be guilt and shame.

I was still young, so my life hadn't gone too far off track yet, but looking back, I can see how God completely changed my direction. I probably would've gotten caught up in partying, chasing popularity, or making choices that would have left me empty. But Jesus saved me early, and He gave my life a new trajectory before I went too far down the wrong path.

From that point on, church became the place I loved to be. I found joy in serving, even alongside people much older than me. It became the centre of my life, and I learned what it meant to truly love life.

Now, as I look towards the future—marriage, work, a family—I believe that life with Jesus is the fullest kind of life. The world tells us to chase success, money, and busyness, but I've learned that God provides what we need.

If I could encourage anyone reading this, it would be this: take time to enjoy the life God's given you. He created opportunities for us to work and to enjoy life. He will always provide. He wants us not just to survive, but to thrive!

Jesus didn't just save me from something—He saved me for something: a life that's real, free, and full of joy.

—Pablo

QUESTIONS FOR REFLECTION

1. What's one part of your life where you've been settling for "less" instead of believing God has more for you?

2. Which negative attitudes (fear, comparison, insecurity) could be blocking your joy right now?

3. What's one way you can intentionally add joy or fun to your week?

4. How much has social media influenced your sense of happiness? What boundaries might help you enjoy life more?

5. How could you help the people around you to enjoy life more and grow closer to God?

NOTES

CHOICE 11

BE A LEADER

There is a leader in you waiting for you
to take the next bold step.

MY STORY

I enrolled in Bible college when I was 19, and I was faithful in my studies. In February, the president of the college came to me and said, "Mel, will you go to Minnedosa, Manitoba, and pastor a church for the summer?"

I said, "I'm not qualified for this. Why have you come to me with this request?"

He replied, "Well, I went to the third-year class, and nobody would go. Then I went to the second-year class, and no one would go. So I've come to you."

"What will it involve?"

"Every Sunday you will teach the adult Bible Class, preach the morning message, lead the Sunday morning service, and conduct the Sunday night service. During the week you can lead a midweek Bible study and a prayer meeting, and—if you would like—start a youth ministry in the church."

I responded, "I am definitely not qualified for this! When do you need an answer?"

"Pray about it and give me the answer tomorrow morning."

I went to my room and knelt by a steam heater. As I prayed, there was the sound of *psst, psst, psst* from the heater. "Lord, is it your plan that I go to Minnedosa to pastor the church there?"

Over and over I asked the Lord the same question, and all I heard was *psst, psst, psst* from the heater. I got up, put on my coat, and said to myself, I must speak to my mother about this.

I walked down the street to the phone booth and inserted coins in the telephone. My mother answered. "Mother," I said, "the president wants me to go and pastor a church in Minnedosa, Manitoba. What do you think?"

She replied, "Son, when you were in my womb, I laid hands on you and dedicated you to the ministry. Go, son, go!"

In that moment, I could hear the voice of my heavenly Father confirming the words my earthly mother had spoken. This wasn't just some impulsive career opportunity. It was a divine commissioning I had been prepared for since before I was born. I knew God wasn't asking me to walk this path alone but had already been preparing me for such a time as this.

The next morning, I told the president that I would accept the assignment, but I needed help. "Sir, will you mentor me and prepare me with messages to go to Minnedosa and do what God is calling me to do?"

He agreed, and Minnedosa became the launchpad for a lifetime of leadership adventures awaiting me as I boldly followed God's calling.

My journey into a life of service began with a step of faith when presented with a unique open door. And the same principle is true for you today: when God provides an opportunity to take the lead and stretch your wings, don't hesitate or doubt your qualifications. Step up, step out, and embrace the challenge He is calling you into!

It may feel overwhelming, and you may wonder if you're ready. But if you're sure it's the Lord's leading, then trust that He has been carefully preparing you every step of the way up until this very moment. Your obedient "yes" will lead to a lifetime of purpose and leadership impact beyond what you can see today.

So, pay attention and be ready for the open doors God will put in front of you. And when that career opportunity, ministry assignment, or leadership role presents itself, don't shrink back in self-doubt or insecurity. Step boldly through those open doors, confident that your ultimate Leader has fully equipped you for the path ahead. You were formed for such a day as this!

STEP UP, STEP OUT, AND STEP INTO

As a Christian, you're called to lead—whether you think of yourself as a leader or not. Leadership isn't just about standing on a platform or running an organization. It's about modelling what it looks like to follow Jesus, whether at school, work, or among friends and family.

Maybe you're thinking, Not me! I'm definitely not leadership material. Perhaps you feel disqualified because you lack education or connections or because of past mistakes. Trust me, we all carry baggage that makes us feel unworthy or incapable. But God specializes in developing unlikely leaders.

When God opens doors for you to step up and lead, don't let those doubts hold you back. Take the first step, even when it feels uncomfortable. Your calling isn't limited by your past or your current abilities. The work will be challenging, but the potential is unlimited. Who knows where God might take you if you're willing to say yes?

I see leadership as being made up of three "steps": step up, step out, and step into.

Step up means maximise the person you are right now. Step out means take action and do something you have never done before. And step into means move into the plan of God. Let's look at each of these a bit deeper.

STEP UP
Maximise the person you are right now

Too often we disqualify ourselves from opportunities because we feel inadequate or unprepared for the role. But God doesn't wait until we have it all together to invite us into His plans. He sees not just who we currently are, but who we can become through His empowering grace.

Stepping up means facing your present season with faith and confidence. Don't compare yourself to others or focus on what you currently lack. Simply be the best version of yourself right now. Develop your existing skills, experiences, perspectives, and spiritual gifts to their fullest potential.

Remember, God doesn't call the qualified—He qualifies the called through the power of His Spirit working in them. Just as He took stammering Moses, fearful Gideon, or the overlooked young shepherd David and shaped them into leaders, He can do the same with you. When you humbly step up and make yourself available, God will supernaturally equip you for the role He's inviting you into.

The Bible repeatedly tells us to maximise who we are in our current season as faithful preparation for greater leadership impact. As the parable in Matthew 25:21 states, "Well done, good and faithful servant! You have been faithful with a few things; I will put you in charge of many things." God is watching how diligently we steward the roles and resources He's entrusted to us right now, no matter how small they may seem.

So how do we do that?

1. *Identify and lean into your strengths.* Your natural talents and spiritual gifts are what the Lord has perfectly equipped you with for this season (2 Timothy 1:7). Don't obsess over your weaknesses. Instead, pour your energies into improving your present capabilities as an encourager,

strategist, creative thinker, or hard worker. There are many tests or assessments you can take to help you discover your abilities, gifts, and strengths.

2. *Consistently develop your skills through practice, even if amateur at first.* The skills needed for leadership like public speaking, task management, and conflict resolution must be sharpened over time. The Bible says in 1 Corinthians 9:25 (ESV), "Every athlete exercises self-control in all things." How much more should we commit to the hard work of stretching and developing ourselves? Every leader has had to take the "natural" talent they have been given and hone it through hours of practice. I've heard it said that in order to master something, you have to spend 10,000 hours practicing it—so get going!

3. *Do everything with excellence and a good work ethic.* "Whatever you do, work at it with all your heart, as working for the Lord" (Colossians 3:23 ESV). When you are reliable and diligent in smaller areas of responsibility, it sets you up for greater kingdom responsibilities. People should be able to trust you to do what you say you will do. Do you have a reputation for being reliable? If not, start today. Begin with the small things, learn and grow, and become excellent in all you do.

4. *Be a continual learner.* Read, listen, watch, find mentors, and study the skills and mindsets required for the areas of influence you feel called to. There are so many books, courses, videos, and resources that can help you. I have read or listened to hundreds of leadership books and many leadership teachings, and I will never stop because growing in our leadership skills is something we can do forever.

5. *Develop emotional and spiritual maturity, not just skills and talents.* As 1 Timothy 4:12 (NIV) teaches, "Set an example for believers in speech, conduct, love, faith and purity." A lifestyle of humility, self-awareness, and care for others is more important than any natural ability.

The more you maximise who you are right now across every area of your life, the more you prepare yourself for future promotion into greater spheres of influence (Luke 16:10). God loves to give the faithful people who "bloom where they are planted" even greater opportunities and responsibilities.

STEP OUT
Take action and do something new.

At its core, stepping out as a leader takes courage. It means leaving the comfort of what you already know and trying something that stretches you. The voice of fear will always try to shut you down: "You're too young. You don't know enough. What if you mess up?" But courage is moving forward anyway. So how do you do that?

1. *Look to young leaders in the Bible.* You're not the first young person God has called. David was still a kid when he faced Goliath. Mary was a teenager when God trusted her with His Son. Timothy had to be reminded not to let anyone look down on his age. God has always used young people who were willing to say yes. God has a long track record of using young people who were willing to courageously follow His lead. Their age was no barrier—only their availability and obedience mattered.

2. *Trust God to equip you.* When God gives you a job to do, He doesn't hand you the assignment and walk away. He gives strength, wisdom, and the gifts you need. You might feel inexperienced, but God fills in the gaps. Think of the boy with the loaves and fish—he just offered what he had, and God did the rest. The talents and provision will follow after that first step of obedience. Watch what He can do when you commit your little to Him.

3. *Stay teachable and keep learning.* When you start something new, you won't know everything—and that's okay. Come in with a humble, teachable attitude. Ask questions. Try things. Learn from mistakes. Leadership isn't learned only from books; it grows through real-life experience. Start where you are, no matter how small, and keep growing.

4. *Find mentors and build your team.* You don't have to go on this leadership journey alone. Look for wise mentors who can guide you and speak honestly into your life. Build a support team of friends and leaders who will encourage you, challenge you, and help sharpen your skills.

5. *Keep your eyes on the vision.* There will be challenges, setbacks, and moments you want to quit. When that happens, go back to the "why." Remember what God called you to do. Keep eternity in mind, and you'll find the strength to keep going. Nothing you do for God is wasted.

Stepping out takes courage, trust, and persistence, but as you keep moving forward, you'll grow into the leader God created you to be. The leadership journey won't always be easy, but it will absolutely be worth it.

STEP INTO

Move into the plan God reveals to you.

Stepping up means walking through open doors, and stepping out means having courage to do new, unfamiliar things. But stepping into your calling is something deeper. It's moving forward with a clear sense of purpose into a role God has already shaped uniquely for you.

It's like wearing a pair of shoes that fit perfectly or putting on a suit made just for you. There's a sense of "I was made for this." God begins revealing your purpose through His leading, circumstances, and those gentle nudges in your spirit.

For some people, stepping into their calling looks like taking on a ministry role or receiving a leadership mantle that's being passed down. For others, it means stepping into something new—a business, a creative path, parenthood, a cause you can't ignore. Whatever it is, it takes spiritual awareness to recognise where God has been pointing you so you can step into that lane with confidence and commitment.

As you do, the confusion starts to lift. What once felt heavy or blurry becomes a sense of hitting God's "bullseye" for this season. When you're aligned with His plan, the grace, strength, and anointing you need are already there.

So when God begins opening new doors of leadership, be ready to step up with what you already have, step out with courage, and step into the purpose He's designed just for you. Stay alert, stay willing, and keep moving forward into the influence and impact He's prepared for your life.

SCRIPTURES ABOUT LEADERSHIP

Joshua 1:9 (NIV)
"Have I not commanded you? Be strong and courageous. Do not be afraid; do not be discouraged, for the Lord your God will be with you wherever you go."

1 Corinthians 16:13–14 (NIV)
"Be on your guard; stand firm in the faith; be courageous; be strong. Do everything in love."

Psalm 78:72 (NIV)
"And David shepherded them with integrity of heart; with skillful hands he led them."

Isaiah 6:8 (NIV)
"Then I heard the voice of the Lord saying, 'Whom shall I send? And who will go for us?' And I said, 'Here am I. Send me!'"

1 Peter 5:2–3 (NIV)
"Be shepherds of God's flock that is under your care... not lording it over those entrusted to you, but being examples to the flock."

Matthew 20:26–28 (NIV)
"...whoever wants to become great among you must be your servant... just as the Son of Man did not come to be served, but to serve, and to give his life as a ransom for many."

Proverbs 11:14 (NIV)
"For lack of guidance a nation falls, but victory is won through many advisers."

YOUR LEADERSHIP JOURNEY STARTS NOW

The journey into leadership isn't just for people who already seem confident or put-together. God loves taking ordinary young people—those who feel inexperienced, unsure, or even marked by a rough past—and shaping them into leaders who make a real difference. Just think of Timothy, David, and so many others who never looked like "the obvious choice."

The key is saying yes to the process God invites you into: first stepping up and using what you already have, then stepping out into new opportunities even when they feel intimidating, and finally stepping into the specific roles and purposes He's been preparing for you all along.

It won't always be easy, but God will strengthen and equip you as you go. So stay faithful in the small things, keep growing in your character and skills, and walk through the doors God opens with courage.

When you feel underqualified or unprepared, turn to God. That's exactly when He loves to show His strength through you. Who knows what adventures and Kingdom impact are ahead if you just take the first steps of obedience today? Your leadership journey starts now.

LEIGH'S STORY

At 21, I dedicated my life to Jesus and was baptized on November 13, 2022. When I told my mother about my decision, she looked at me, puzzled, and said, "Why? You were already baptized as a baby."

I grew up in a Catholic household, so Jesus wasn't entirely unfamiliar. But I was Catholic in name only, not in faith. If you had seen how I lived from age sixteen to nineteen, you wouldn't believe I'd ever heard the Word of God. My life was far from godly. As a young student-athlete, I became influential and popular. At 16, I was the first among my teammates and friends to have a girlfriend, and I felt on top of the world. By 17, I had my first alcoholic drink, threw my first party with over 100 people, and started smoking weed when it was still illegal, which made me feel even cooler.

What began as an experiment turned into a small hustle— buying weed online and selling it to others. As I got older, my recklessness intensified, spiraling out of control. By 19, I was so broken that I attempted to take my own life by driving my car off a cliff. By God's grace, I lost control of the vehicle before reaching the edge and crashed into the woods. Miraculously, I emerged unscathed, though the weight of my brokenness was overwhelming.

I was utterly lost. Then, on October 9, 2022, Jesus met me where I was. His love moved in my life in ways I could hardly describe, overwhelming me with grace despite my past. Standing at the altar at Home Church, I found myself weeping uncontrollably as a pastor prayed over me. In that same season, I made a life-changing choice: I committed the next three years to God by enrolling in Bible college.

"Enter by the narrow gate; for wide is the gate and broad is the way that leads to destruction, and there are many who go in by it" (Matthew 7:13, NKJV). This verse became my anchor during my years at Bible college. While my peers pursued traditional paths in universities, I chose an unconventional road, trusting God's will for my life. That choice to follow the narrow gate, though daunting, filled me with purpose and strength.

Stepping into God's calling, I began serving in youth ministry without being asked. I showed up, offered my help, and soon found myself leading naturally. Each step deepened my transformation, reshaping my identity from the broken teenager I once was into the person God created me to be.

Another verse guided me: *"For to be carnally minded is death, but to be spiritually minded is life and peace"* (Romans 8:6, NKJV). This truth renewed my mind, brightened my perspective, and filled me with the Holy Spirit's peace, guiding me towards a life of purpose. Now, at 24, I've graduated with a degree in Christian Ministries, own a business, and lead in my church with a burning passion for Christ.

In November 2024, I was blessed with an opportunity to join a mission trip to Africa, serving at the Home of Hope Dream Centre in Rwanda and Kenya. There, I preached at youth conferences, shared my testimony with congregations, and led hundreds to Christ. This unforgettable experience showed me the power of choosing to follow God's call, as my story of redemption inspired others to find hope in Him.

The pivotal choices I made early in my young adult life—choosing faith over despair and purpose over popularity—allowed Christ's love to pull me from a pit of hopelessness and set me on a path of eternal purpose.

—Leigh

QUESTIONS FOR REFLECTION

1. Do you see yourself the way God sees you—as someone with purpose and influence? Why or why not?

2. What is one leadership opportunity in front of you where you could step up, step out, and step into?

3. Who could mentor you or help you grow in leadership? Have you asked them?

4. If someone followed your example this week, where would it lead them?

5. What are some ways to overcome negativity and have the courage you need to lead?

NOTES

CHOICE 12

WIN AND NEVER QUIT

Why be a loser when you can be a winner?

MY STORY

As I was shaking hands with hundreds of people at a major speaking conference, a person said to me, "Pastor, how is it possible that for fifty years you have been faithful to lead at Home Church, first as the founding pastor and now on the team serving your son Jachin and giving oversight to churches around the world? That's a major accomplishment. How did you do it?"

My answer was, "When things got really difficult, Heather and I chose not to quit like many pastors do. And when life was wonderful, we didn't want to quit!"

The key to having a winning life is: "Choose not to quit. Be faithful, be loyal, and choose to win." People want a fancy formula, but often it's just the decision not to quit which is the key to your success.

John the apostle was the writer of the Book of Revelation. When the Romans tried to kill him by boiling him in hot oil, he would not burn. So history tells us they banished him to the island of Patmos, where God gave him a vision and a message to seven important churches. Every church had a different set of problems, from persecution to bad doctrines to circumstances that were very difficult. But the message was the same to every church. He wrote simply: "Overcome."

To overcome means to rise above all odds that work against you and to win, win, win! Here are some promises that God has for you:

- God is my light and my salvation (Psalm 27:1).
- God's Word is a lamp for my feet and a light for my path (Psalm 119:105).
- God is my shepherd (Psalm 23:1).
- God is my stronghold (Psalm 9:9).
- God is my refuge in times of trouble (Psalm 46:1).
- God is my strength and my shield (Psalm 28:7).
- God is on my side (Psalm 118:6).

The good news is that you can stand on the Word of God, face your giants in life, and win. David faced the bear and the lion, then ran towards the giant Goliath, hit him with a stone from a sling, cut off the giant's head with his own sword, and won a great victory for Israel. You can win too!

In life, there will be financial challenges, relationship challenges, family challenges, and every kind of challenge. Let your choice be to stay faithful, loyal, and committed to God, and overcome by your faith.

In our journey, Heather and I have faced every kind of obstacle you can imagine. There were seasons when we could barely make the church mortgage payment. Times when city permits for our building seemed impossible to obtain. Moments when relationships with key leaders became strained. Through it all, we learned one crucial lesson: Winners don't quit, and quitters don't win.

I remember one particularly difficult season when we were facing multiple challenges at once. The easy thing would have been to throw in the towel and say, "Maybe we're not cut out for this." But that's when I would open my Bible to read about Paul in that Roman prison. Here was a man who had been beaten, flogged, and chained, yet he wrote, "I have learned to be content whatever the circumstances" (Philippians 4:11 NIV).

Paul didn't just survive his trials; he thrived in them! While chained in his prison cell, he wrote letters that would encourage believers for generations to come. He declared, "I can do all things through Christ who strengthens me" (Philippians 4:13 NKJV). That's the spirit of an overcomer!

This means more than just barely hanging on and hoping things get better. It means standing firmly on God's promises even when everything around you says to quit. When the challenges come—and they will—you have a choice: let them bury you, or let them build you. Why be a loser when you can be a winner? Choose to win!

FAITH IN ADVERSITY

Whatever you do, don't quit! Instead, stir up your faith. "Faith it until you make it." Faith is your ability to believe, to stay strong, to look forward, to conquer and overcome, to remain consistent. Faith and endurance go together, because when you believe the promises of God, that faith enables you to push through difficulties and pain that lie in the way of those promises. That's why the author of Hebrews encourages us to "follow the example of those who are going to inherit God's promises because of their faith and endurance" (Hebrews 6:12 NLT).

The difficulties we face fall into three different categories, as we learn from the life of Apostle Paul in Acts 27–28. In the story, Paul is caught in a violent storm on his way to Rome and the ship is eventually wrecked. Everyone survives by swimming to shore and ends up on the island of Malta. But then, while Paul is helping build a fire, he is bitten by a venomous snake. Instead of dying, though, he shakes off the snake without any harm and soon preaches about Jesus to the entire island.

Notice the three things Paul faced: storms, shipwrecks, and snakebites. Let's talk about each of these as a metaphor for the situations you'll come across in life.

Storms

The storms of life have a way of blowing in suddenly and with incredible force, threatening to capsize our faith and send us crashing onto the rocks of doubt, fear, and despair. A family member's illness, a broken relationship, a dream turned to ashes. Just when you thought you were sailing smoothly, a hurricane-force squall rises out of nowhere.

It's in those wave-pounding moments when true faith gets tested and proven. Can you stay upright and on course when the winds howl violently against your life? The key is staying connected to the eternal truths of God's Word. Let His truth be your anchor, your rudder, and your compass.

The good news is that no storm lasts forever. They eventually blow over. So, keep the promises of Scripture in your heart and mind. Keep rejecting the lies and negativity trying to flood your thoughts. If you'll just "faith it until you make it," the clouds will part and tranquil waters will return.

Shipwrecks

Sometimes the crises we face aren't temporary storms but more like full-on shipwrecks. The vessel carrying your hopes and dreams has been smashed against the rocks. Maybe a relationship has been irreparably broken. An opportunity you were counting on has disintegrated, leaving you adrift. A family member passes away. The ship you were sailing on is now splintered wreckage.

It's okay to admit the cold reality of these tragedies and to call a shipwreck a shipwreck. Don't try to pretend away the pain or downplay how bad the situation is through empty words. Let grief happen authentically and naturally. In fact, this is where faith begins—with being honest about your circumstances.

But faith doesn't stop with honesty. It starts there, then it moves forward into the open waters of God's purpose and plan. Like Paul and the other passengers who had to start swimming or clinging to debris, your faith calls you to let go of the shattered remains of what once was and start paddling and kicking furiously towards the shore of what can still be. The shipwreck may have changed your circumstances, but it doesn't get to ruin your destiny.

So, grieve what was lost, but don't drown in sorrow. The beach of "new beginnings, resurrection, and better things ahead" is not far off if you'll just keep faithing it. The shipwreck is a brutal turning point, but it's not the end of your life's story. Keep swimming!

Snakebites

Even after surviving the shipwrecks and storms, life still has a way of hitting us with painful opposition. Just like Paul getting bitten by a viper on Malta right after making it through the storm and wreck, we sometimes can't even sit by the fire without something else coming at us. Betrayals, injustices, attacks, failures, setbacks, harsh words—these are the "snakebites" that make us question God's presence and protection.

But Paul didn't get caught up in the islanders' shock or curiosity. He simply shook the snake into the fire. He knew that no attack from darkness could stop what God was doing. It's an incredible picture of steady, persevering faith. The snakebites may sting for a moment, but when you stay focused on God's light and calling, their venom loses its power.

That's the kind of steady, unshaken faith we're invited to live out. When the snake tries to sink its fangs in, shake it off and keep moving forward. Yes, deal with the attack when it comes—but don't let it stop you or freeze you in fear. Challenges will always show up in a life that's lived for something bigger than itself.

Paul's response of faith—and God's protection—opened the door of faith for the people on the island. In the same way, your ability to persevere in tough moments will open doors for you. People will see your faith and the power of God at work in your life.

SCRIPTURES ABOUT WINNING AND NOT QUITTING

Galatians 6:9 (NIV)
"Let us not become weary in doing good, for at the proper time we will reap a harvest if we do not give up."

Hebrews 12:1 (NIV)
"Therefore, since we are surrounded by such a great cloud of witnesses, let us throw off everything that hinders and the sin that so easily entangles. And let us run with perseverance the race marked out for us."

1 Corinthians 15:58 (NIV)
"Therefore, my dear brothers and sisters, stand firm. Let nothing move you. Always give yourselves fully to the work of the Lord, because you know that your labour in the Lord is not in vain."

2 Corinthians 4:8–9 (NIV)

"We are hard pressed on every side, but not crushed; perplexed, but not in despair; persecuted, but not abandoned; struck down, but not destroyed."

Romans 5:3–4 (NIV)

"Not only so, but we also glory in our sufferings, because we know that suffering produces perseverance; perseverance, character; and character, hope."

James 1:12 (NIV)

"Blessed is the one who perseveres under trial because, having stood the test, that person will receive the crown of life that the Lord has promised to those who love him."

Joshua 1:9 (NIV)

"Have I not commanded you? Be strong and courageous. Do not be afraid; do not be discouraged, for the Lord your God will be with you wherever you go."

THE UPSIDE OF FAITH

"Faithing it" isn't just a matter of gritting your teeth and waiting out the storm. It's about believing that good will come through that dark, difficult thing you are facing. Faith means remembering that God has not abandoned you even when you feel alone. It means trusting that the long-term results of remaining faithful will outweigh the temporary pain of the struggle.

When you look at challenges through the eyes of faith, you realise that they are working to your advantage. We don't need to seek out suffering, obviously, and God doesn't expect us to pretend to enjoy it when it comes. That would be strange. But He does remind us that He works all things together for our good (Romans 8:28). In God's hands, even the painful parts of life ultimately benefit us in some way.

The apostle James wrote:

"Dear brothers and sisters, when troubles of any kind come your way, consider it an opportunity for great joy. For you know that when your faith is tested, your endurance has a chance to grow. So let it grow, for when your endurance is fully developed, you will be perfect and complete, needing nothing." (James 1:2-4 NLT)

Going through hard times will make you a better person if you face them with courage and wisdom. That's not easy; but it's not impossible, either. Remember, you were made for this. You are ready for it. You will be good at it. When you respond the right way to trouble, trouble does not take you down, but rather it makes you greater.

You were created by God with the ability to not only withstand pressure, but to grow through it. To overcome it. To use it to your advantage. Don't give up when you face difficulties, and don't get frustrated with God. Instead, turn to God and let Him remind you of who you are. Find the strength of God within your heart and stay the course.

HOW TO FAITH IT UNTIL YOU MAKE IT

While I can't give you a roadmap to walk through every possible difficulty, I can tell you what I've learned about "just faithing it" through the craziness of life. Remember, faith is your friend. It is your compass in the storm, your life jacket in shipwrecks, and your medicine for snakebites. So, what does it mean to "just faith it"?

Faith Sees

Paul writes in 2 Corinthians 5:7, "For we walk by faith, not by sight" (NKJV). What we perceive with our five senses is not the sum total of reality. Faith is our ability to see what isn't visible and to know what can't be proven. Faith is the sixth sense that gives us the ability to believe for the impossible in the middle of a storm.

Living by faith means taking steps based not just on what your human self perceives, but also what your spiritual self perceives. Before you make important decisions, always take time to listen to faith. Learn to see the world around you through the lens of unshakeable trust in God.

Faith Walks

The verse we just read says that we "walk by faith." That word walk reminds us that faith keeps moving forward. It might be slow, but it's sure. Don't stress out if your steps forward seem small and unexciting. Just keep walking in faith, love, and obedience. One day, like the old story of the tortoise and the hare, you'll find yourself at the finish line, looking back with pride and joy at your amazing accomplishments.

Faith Stands

In the Bible, there are many examples of people standing firm in their faith despite facing incredible opposition and obstacles. Daniel kept praying to God even when it was outlawed. Shadrach,

Meshach, and Abednego refused to bow to the statue of gold, even when threatened with death in a fiery furnace. The apostles preached the Gospel boldly in the face of beatings, imprisonments, and death threats.

When the storms of life come crashing in and the winds of adversity howl all around you, faith is what allows you to stand firm and not waver or back down. Yes, you might get battered by the winds. Yes, the ground might shake violently under your feet. But if your life is built on the solid rock of God's truth, you won't be swept away. Stay standing!

Faith Endures

Sometimes our problems don't just disappear. There are hard seasons and difficult situations that don't simply go away. Faith is what allows us to stay hopeful over the long haul, anchoring our soul in the unbreakable promises of God's Word.

When it feels like your faith is about to disappear, reach out and grab those promises like a lifeline. Let their truth fill you with hope and strength. The God who guided Noah, Abraham, Moses, David, and Paul will guide you too if you will endure.

Faith Overcomes

At the end of the day, faith is what overcomes. It overcomes fear, doubt, sin, the devil, and every other obstacle that wants to derail you from God's best path for your life. The apostle John wrote, "For every child of God defeats this evil world, and we achieve this victory through our faith" (1 John 5:4 NLT). Faith connects you to the same power that raised Christ from the dead. It unleashes miracles into the natural realm. It gives you authority over darkness. Don't ever underestimate the explosive force of a Christ-follower who refuses to quit or compromise. The great revivalist Charles Finney once said, "Nothing is accomplished in this world until someone plants themselves on the promises of God, and refuses to give up." Do that, and you'll become an unstoppable overcomer!

DECIDE TO WIN!

As you navigate the storms, shipwrecks, and snakebites that come your way in life, don't panic. You were made for this. You have what it takes to stay the course and refuse to quit. Just keep faithing it, as my wife and I have done for over fifty years of ministry on the front line.

Now, I can look back and see how those intense trials and tests were refining our faith and perseverance for the long haul. We learned to be faith survivors in those early years. We drew our strength from Scripture's promises about not growing weary or losing heart. We kept our eyes locked on Jesus, the champion of our faith who endured far worse suffering and testing. Who were we to quit when the God who raised the dead was on our side?

And you know what? The little church we started in Red Deer, Alberta eventually broke through and became a mighty move of God's Spirit. Souls were saved, lives transformed, leaders raised up to spark more works. Many more locations were started, and today tens of thousands of people gather all over the world to worship Jesus in Home Church locations. It wasn't by our power, but by stubbornly remaining present and keeping faith against all odds. If you don't quit, you win in the end.

So I encourage you: You are more than a conqueror through Christ who keeps empowering you. Stay the course, shake off the vipers, and keep faithing it no matter what comes against you. Your brightest days and greatest victories are just ahead if you refuse to quit. Decide now to win, win, win!

KAI'S STORY

Hi, my name is Kai. I grew up in Edmonton, Alberta, in a home filled with faith, prayer, and the sound of missionary stories. My parents had a deep heart for the nations and a burning passion to serve God wherever He called them. When I was five years old, that calling took us across the world to Romania. My dad had founded several orphanages through an organization called C.A.I.R.D—Children's Aid International Relief and Development, and what was supposed to be a few months abroad turned into something that would shape the rest of my life.

Just three weeks after we arrived, my father's best friend, Derek Mann—the director who was meant to take over the orphanages—was suddenly diagnosed with a terminal brain tumor. He returned to Canada and passed away within weeks. My parents were faced with a choice: return home and leave the work unfinished, or stay and trust God to provide. They prayed, and God spoke clearly—we were to stay.

At five years old, I didn't understand the magnitude of that decision. I just knew that my entire world had been turned upside down. I missed my grandparents, my friends, my language, my familiar life in Canada. I was angry. I refused to learn Romanian for years because, in my heart, I didn't want to belong there.

But God has a way of softening even the most stubborn hearts. Around age eight or nine, I decided to stop fighting my circumstances and start embracing them. I learned Romanian fluently, grew up in the mountain villages, and learned to live like the locals—simple, hardworking, full of faith. My father planted churches, and I became both a missionary kid and a pastor's kid. I loved God deeply. I read my Bible, prayed daily, and wanted to be first in everything I did for Him.

Then my teenage years came—and I lost my way. Many of the boys I knew started getting into drugs, alcohol, and pornography. I followed them. I began living a double life: the perfect pastor's kid on Sunday, and a completely different person the rest of the week. I hid it all, smiled through the guilt, and slowly began to despise the very God I once loved. I didn't want to go to church, I didn't want to attend camps, and I definitely didn't want to follow my father's footsteps anymore.

When I was seventeen, my dad told me I had to attend a regional youth camp. I argued and resisted, but eventually I went, although reluctantly. That week, I was rebellious and disruptive, to the point that my dad and the leaders almost kicked me out. On the final night, everything changed.

The speaker asked each of us to draw a picture of a person and then we were each handed a written story to go with it. The story was of that person's life, and it either ended up on the right side of the board (for those who followed God) or the left (for those who didn't). Out of fifty or sixty stories, only about 5 ended up on the right. I was zoned out, and mine ended up on the left side. But then my father stood up and said, "You might think those were just stories, but that was my youth group. Those were my friends. And now all these years later, only a handful are following God. Where will you be in ten years? Will you follow God or fall away?"

That question hit me like a brick wall. I broke down and wept. That night, I repented. I gave my life back to Jesus and was baptized. It was the moment my story changed—when God took my life and gave it a complete course correct.

From then on, my heart burned to serve Him. At eighteen, I became the children's pastor in Romania. At nineteen, the youth

pastor. At twenty, our church's camp director. I had found my purpose again.

During that same season, I began studying Digital Media and
Graphic Design through the University of Calgary. I had always
loved creativity, photography, and storytelling. After completing
two years online, I came to Calgary in 2019 to finish my degree. My
plan was simple: return to Romania, take over my father's ministry,
and continue building the vision. But God had a different plan.

One morning in prayer, I asked God what He wanted from my
life. His answer was so clear it shook me: "Kai, I am calling you back
to Canada. I'm calling you into business. You will return in September of 2020."

I didn't understand it at all. My parents were upset at first—
until God confirmed it separately to both of them through a dream
and a vision. So, in obedience, I prepared to leave Romania after
living there for eighteen years.

The timing couldn't have been stranger. COVID hit. The year
2020 was a storm. While visiting South Africa with my family that
spring, the pandemic escalated, and we were trapped under mili-
tary lockdown for nearly four months—surrounded by barbed wire
fences and armed patrols. It was one of the darkest seasons of my
life. Yet even there, God spoke to me again. He said: "Kai, your
attitude in the valley will define the altitude of your blessings."

Those words became my anchor. When I finally returned to
Canada, I was determined that my attitude, regardless of the circumstances, had to remain anchored on Christ.

September was rapidly approaching and doors were closing
everywhere. Yet I obeyed. I landed in Didsbury, Alberta with just
$500 and a single suitcase. I was a broke 22-year-old missionary kid
with no idea how "business" would ever fit into my calling.

Then the miracles began. Within 24 hours of arriving, I
received a call from a local businessman who needed a graphic
designer—the very role I was trained for. Within a week, I was

invited to Home Church Mountain View, where I immediately felt loved and accepted. Within two weeks, someone that hadn't seen me in years said they had a dream from the Lord to give me one of their cars! Within days, I had a job, a car, and a place to live—all things I couldn't have provided for myself.

In 2022, I took a leap of faith and started M.Media, my own media company, after being encouraged by Mike Bolton at a Success Builders meeting. Within two months, my income doubled. Within a year, I hired my first employee—a young man I had mentored through Home Church. The next year, I hired another. Then another. By 2025, I had a full team of five, all of whom I had personally discipled or served alongside in church.

What began as a dream with $500 and faith has grown into a thriving company that's on track to gross $1 million next year. But more important than the numbers is the testimony that God truly honours obedience, generosity, and perseverance.

Last year at Success Builders, Ryan challenged us to "Make a goal and work at it like never before for 30 days." I wrote down a goal: to make $10,000 in one month so I could tithe $1,000. I thought tithing $1000 was crazy. But I wanted to do it. I worked hard, prayed hard, and at the end of that month, I'd earned $12,000. My mind was blown. I never thought it possible. I joyfully tithed $1,200 to my church, the most meaningful gift I'd ever given. Since then, I've continued giving, tithing, and bringing first fruits each week—starting small, but watching God multiply it again and again.

Home Church and Success Builders have completely transformed my life. They taught me that faith and perseverance are the cornerstones of victory. That storms, shipwrecks, and setbacks don't stop your destiny—they shape it.

Today, I live by a simple life motto: "Discipleship through Entrepreneurship." My dream is to use business as a tool for mentoring and discipling young men, helping them discover their purpose, rise in faith, and win at life by never quitting.

God took a stubborn missionary kid who once ran from his calling and turned him into a man who builds others up through that same calling. Every challenge—every valley, every loss, every moment of doubt—became part of the testimony that proves this truth: When you don't quit, you win. And when you win through faith, God gets the glory.

—Kai

DISCUSSION QUESTIONS

1. When have you felt like quitting, and what helped you keep going?

2. What storms, shipwrecks, or snakebites are you facing right now?

3. What promise from God do you need to hold onto in this season?

4. How can you "keep walking" in faith even if your steps feel small?

5. What would "winning" look like for you this week?

NOTES

CONCLUSION
MY CHOICE

It's time to make a decision.

You Choose is all about making the right decisions for your future, and I trust that as you've read the stories of my life, taken in the Biblical truths, and shared in the testimonies of each of the young adults, you've been inspired and challenged to make good choices in your own life.

It all starts with the most important decision you'll ever make: choosing to follow Christ and live according to His Word.

My grandson Jude is one of the finest youth leaders at Home Church. He is a great example to follow, and below he shares his story of how he made a commitment to be "All In" for Christ.

JUDE'S STORY

Hi, my name is Jude. I'm the son of Jachin and Becca Mullen, pastors of Home Church in Red Deer, Alberta.

Growing up, I became a believer in Jesus and invited him into my life at seven years old, and I was baptized with one of my closest friends, Addison. When I was fourteen, I attended a youth camp, where I realised that I had to choose to go "All In" for my commitment to Christ so that I could fulfil my calling. I fell on my knees and started praying and suddenly I felt God's peace. That was a radical moment when I really made a decision to follow Christ.

After the first week of making that all-In commitment, I started sharing with friends and bringing them to youth. Now, they are following Jesus too.

As you finish reading this book, I invite you to receive Jesus into your life and make the same commitment to Christ that I made. Your life will never be the same!

—Jude

The "All In" commitment, making Jesus the Lord of my life:

1. I choose to live in God's perfect will for my life.
2. I choose to be the person God has created me to be.
3. I choose obedience to God and His Word.
4. I choose to surround myself with good friends and relationships.
5. I choose to live a morally pure life.
6. I choose to live in truth.
7. I choose to live with a mindset of "more than enough."
8. I choose to have good disciplines that shape my future.
9. I choose to be confident.
10. I choose the enjoyment of life as my way of living.
11. I choose to maximise my leadership and step into my calling.
12. I choose to win and never quit!

Date _____

Signature _____

31 CONFESSIONS
OF A WINNER

1. God Has Big Plans for Me.
Jeremiah 29:11 (NIV) — "For I know the plans I have for you," declares the LORD, "plans to prosper you and not to harm you, plans to give you hope and a future."

2. Greatness Is My Future.
Genesis 12:2 (NKJV) — "I will bless you and make your name great; And you shall be a blessing."

3. I Am Who God Says I Am.
Romans 8:16 (NKJV) — "...heirs of God and joint heirs with Christ."

4. I Am Righteous.
2 Corinthians 5:21 (NIV) — "God made him who had no sin to be sin for us, so that in him we might become the righteousness of God."

5. I Have Dominion – I Take Dominion.
Genesis 1:28 (MSG) — "God blessed them: 'Prosper! Reproduce! Fill Earth! Take charge! Be responsible...'"

6. Leadership Is My "Way of Life."
Deuteronomy 28:13 (NLT) — "If you listen to these commands of the LORD your God that I am giving you today, and if you carefully obey them, the LORD will make you the head and not the tail, and you will always be at the top and never at the bottom."

7. God Has Given Me Land to Possess.

Genesis 14:19 (ESV) — "And he blessed him and said, 'Blessed be Abram by God Most High, Possessor of heaven and earth.'"

8. I Take Faith Steps – I Prosper.

Joshua 1:3 (NIV) — "I will give you every place where you set your foot, as I promised Moses."

Psalm 1:3 (NKJV) — "He shall be like a tree planted by the rivers of water... whatever he does shall prosper."

9. I Have Fearless Courage.

Judges 6:12 (ESV) — "And the angel of the LORD appeared to him and said to him, 'The LORD is with you, O mighty man of valor.'"

10. I Have No Fear.

2 Timothy 1:6–7 (NKJV) — "...God has not given us a spirit of fear, but of power and of love and of a sound mind."

11. Courage – Strength – Obedience – Success.

Joshua 1:6–7 (NLT) — "Be strong and very courageous. Be careful to obey all the instructions Moses gave you. Do not deviate from them, turning either to the right or to the left. Then you will be successful in everything you do."

12. I Can, Yes I Can, God Says I Can.

Philippians 4:13 (NKJV) — "I can do all things through Christ who strengthens me."

13. I Am Well Able.

Numbers 13:30 (AMP) — "Caleb quieted the people before Moses and said, 'Let us go up at once and take possession of the land, for we are well able to conquer it.'"

14. Giants Are My Daily Bread.

Numbers 14:8–10 (AMP) — "If the LORD delights in us, then He will bring us into this land and give it to us, a land flowing with milk and honey... only do not rebel... nor fear the people of the land, for they are bread for us... the LORD is with us; do not fear them."

15. When I Pray It! And Say It! I Have It!

Mark 11:23–24 (NKJV) — "For assuredly, I say to you, whoever says to this mountain, 'Be removed and be cast into the sea,' and does not doubt in his heart, but believes that those things he says will come to pass, he will have whatever he says. Therefore I say to you, whatever things you ask when you pray, believe that you receive them, and you will have them."

16. Plans – Paths – Directed by the Lord.

Proverbs 3:5–6 (NLT) — "Trust in the LORD with all your heart; do not depend on your own understanding. Seek his will in all you do, and he will show you which path to take."

17. "YES" Is My Future.

Acts 16:6–10 (NLT) — "...The Holy Spirit prevented them from preaching the word in the province of Asia at that time... the Spirit of Jesus did not allow them to go there... 'Come over to Macedonia and help us!' So we decided to leave at once... having concluded that God was calling us..."

18. God Is with Me.

Exodus 33:14 (NLT) — "The LORD replied, 'I will personally go with you... I will give you rest—everything will be fine for you.'"

19. I Live in God's Favour.
Psalm 30:5 (NLT) — "For his anger lasts only a moment, but his favour lasts a lifetime! Weeping may last through the night, but joy comes with the morning."

20. I Have Double for Every Trouble.
Job 42:12 (AMP) — "The LORD blessed the latter days of Job more than his beginning; for he had fourteen thousand sheep, six thousand camels, one thousand yoke of oxen, and one thousand female donkeys."

21. I Have Joy in Every Trial.
James 1:2 (NLT) — "Dear brothers and sisters, when troubles of any kind come your way, consider it an opportunity for great joy."

22. Endurance Makes Me a Better Person.
James 1:3–4 (NLT) — "...for you know that when your faith is tested, your endurance has a chance to grow. So let it grow, for when your endurance is fully developed, you will be perfect and complete, needing nothing."

23. The Heavens Are Opened and I Am Blessed, Blessed, Blessed.
Malachi 3:10 (NLT) — "'Bring all the tithes into the storehouse so there will be enough food in my Temple. If you do,' says the LORD of Heaven's Armies, 'I will open the windows of heaven for you. I will pour out a blessing so great you won't have enough room to take it in! Try it! Put me to the test!'"

24. God Is My Abundant Provider.
Philippians 4:19 (NKJV) — "And my God shall supply all your needs according to His riches in glory by Christ Jesus."

25. I Will Live in the Land of 'More Than Enough.'
Numbers 14:8 (AMP) — "If the LORD delights in us, then He will bring us into this land and give it to us, a land which flows with milk and honey."

26. My Harvest Is Coming.
Galatians 6:7–9 (NKJV) — "Do not be deceived, God is not mocked; for whatever a man sows, that he will also reap… And let us not grow weary while doing good, for in due season we shall reap if we do not lose heart."

27. I Add Character — I Will Never Fall.
2 Peter 1:3–10 (NLT) — "By his divine power, God has given us everything we need for living a godly life… He has given us great and precious promises… supplement your faith with a generous provision of moral excellence… knowledge… self-control… patient endurance… godliness… brotherly affection… and love for every-one… Do these things, and you will never fall away."

28. I Live in Divine Health.
1 Peter 2:24 (NIV) — "He himself bore our sins in his body on the cross, so that we might die to sins and live for righteousness; 'by his wounds you have been healed.'"
3 John 2 (NIV) — "Dear friend, I pray that you may enjoy good health and that all may go well with you, even as your soul is get-ting along well."

29. I Live a Limitless Life.
Mark 10:27 (NLT) — "Humanly speaking, it is impossible. But not with God. Everything is possible with God."

30. I Am Protected.
Psalm 91:10–11 (NLT) — "No evil will conquer you; no plague will come near your home. For he will order his angels to protect you wherever you go."

31. God Starts – God Finishes.
Philippians 1:6 (NLT) — "And I am certain that God, who began the good work within you, will continue his work until it is finally finished on the day when Christ Jesus returns."

ABOUT THE AUTHOR

Mel is passionate about seeing the next generation make healthy choices in their relationship with Jesus, devoting their lives to His Word, and His Church. Mel and his wife, Heather, live in Red Deer, AB, Canada, where they founded Home Church in 1972. Today, the church is a multi-site, multi-ethnic, and multi-generational church with lead Pastor, Jachin Mullen.

Mel and Heather travel extensively to international Home Church locations, as well as leading conferences and leadership events in the larger body of Christ. Their vision is to empower young people to reach their potential and fulfil their calling. Mel and Heather are blessed with two children—Jachin and his wife, Becca, and Christy and her husband, Chad—and seven amazing grandkids.

They love Jesus, they love their family, and they love the Church!

Other books by this author:
- *Be a Man*
- *Experience Jesus and His Church*
- *OnetoOne*

www.ingramcontent.com/pod-product-compliance
Lightning Source LLC
Chambersburg PA
CBHW051419090426
42737CB00014B/2738

9 781963 127485